Practical Shape

Practical Shape

A Theory of Practical Reasoning

Jonathan Dancy

OXFORD
UNIVERSITY PRESS

OXFORD
UNIVERSITY PRESS

Great Clarendon Street, Oxford, OX2 6DP,
United Kingdom

Oxford University Press is a department of the University of Oxford.
It furthers the University's objective of excellence in research, scholarship,
and education by publishing worldwide. Oxford is a registered trade mark of
Oxford University Press in the UK and in certain other countries

The moral rights of the author have been asserted

First Edition published in 2018
Impression: 1

Published in the United States of America by Oxford University Press
198 Madison Avenue, New York, NY 10016, United States of America

British Library Cataloguing in Publication Data
Data available

Library of Congress Control Number: 2018931630

ISBN 978-0-19-880544-1

Printed and bound by
CPI Group (UK) Ltd, Croydon, CR0 4YY

For SARAH, finally.

Contents

Detailed Contents

Acknowledgements

I start with thanks for useful suggestions or conversations—which the individuals involved may well now have forgotten but I have not—to Maria Alvarez, David Bakhurst, Akeel Bilgrami, John Broome, Ray Buchanan, Arthur Collins, Sinan Dogramaci, Matt Evans, Christopher Hookway, Susanne Mantel, Daniel Muñoz, Peter Railton, Joseph Raz, Debbie Roberts, Mark Sainsbury, Miriam Schoenfield, James Sherman, Michael Smith, David Sosa, Bart Streumer, Jay Wallace, and Daniel Wodak.

More generally, I am extremely grateful to various groups. First were the groups who attended the graduate classes I taught on this material in its first draft at Princeton (2014) and then at UT Austin and at Reading (both in 2015). Then there was the group at Queen's University, Kingston, Ontario, who under David Bakhurst's leadership read the same first draft and devoted considerable time to writing detailed responses as they went along, and then spent a whole weekend explaining it all to me in March 2016. Finally there were the participants in a three-day workshop on a nearly final draft at Saarbrücken in Germany in July 2017.

And I owe special thanks to some individuals who read the entire work in some form or other and gave me enormously helpful comments in the later stages: the three referees for OUP, most especially Kurt Sylvan, whose combined reports served very much as a wake-up call, and after that to John Schwenkler.

I am also very grateful to the College of Liberal Arts at the University of Texas at Austin for the award of a College Fellowship in 2014, which gave me a semester's research leave, and thereby enabled me to produce a complete initial draft; without this I might never have managed really to get going.

I owe a quite different debt of gratitude to my wife Sarah for her love and support throughout my career, sustained in these, its now closing stages. This book, which I intend to be my last, is dedicated to her.

JD

Introduction

. . . I require that the critique of a pure practical reason, if it is to be carried through completely, be able at the same time to present the unity of practical with speculative reason in a common principle, since there can, in the end, be only one and the same reason, which must be distinguished merely in its application.

(Kant, *Groundwork of the Metaphysics of Morals* 4.391 tr. Gregor)

0.1 Practical Reasoning

In this book I present a general account of reasoning, which stresses the similarities between practical reasoning and what I will call theoretical reasoning; the latter is reasoning to belief, the former is reasoning to action. The focus of my account is, however, on the practical. I maintain that if we start our enquiries into reasoning by thinking about theoretical reasoning, as theorists so often have started, we will end up with a distorted conception of practical reasoning—if, indeed, we do not end up denying the very possibility of such a thing. Many have maintained that reasoning is *as such* a passage from beliefs to beliefs, and that the consequence of this is that we cannot reason to action, either directly or indirectly. We cannot do it directly because we can only reason directly to beliefs. And we cannot do it indirectly because once we have reasoned to beliefs, there is nothing more for reasoning to do; we cannot hope to take those beliefs and reason from them to action. So the only thing that practical reasoning could be is reasoning to a conclusion that is practically relevant, a conclusion such as 'I ought to F', or 'I have good reason to F'. One may act in the light of such a conclusion, but any move to action takes place after reasoning has finished doing its official job.

I maintain, however, with Kant (at least if we are to take the epigraph to this chapter at face value), that reasoning can be practical in a stronger sense than the previous paragraph allows. The 'unity of practical with speculative reason' is not the idea that all practical reason is really speculative reason in the service of a practical purpose, but the idea that there is a common core to practical reasoning and speculative (which I am calling theoretical) reasoning, and that speculative reasoning is not that core. I will offer an account of reasoning in general that applies equally well to reasoning to belief and to reasoning to action. And, as we will see, there are other forms of reasoning than these. Many have held that there can be reasoning to intention, and that this is not merely a special form of reasoning to belief. But there can also be reasoning from doubt to doubt, from belief to doubt, from hope to hope, from hope to fear, and so on. My account of reasoning should apply to them all, if it is to prove capable of covering the ground intended. (And there are difficulties for me here, which I try to confront in 7.9.)

But if my account were true, we would expect that there is no uniquely right place to start in the study of reasoning—that one would not need, for instance, to start as I do with the practical and work from there to the theoretical. I claim, however, that theorists have almost universally worked in the other direction, and that in doing so they have imposed misconceived ideas that stemmed from mistakes they had already made on the other side, in their thinking about theoretical reasoning. Since it is much harder to impose on one's conception of the theoretical any mistakes one has made antecedently on the practical side, I maintain that we do better to start by thinking about practical reason, and only later apply the ideas that emerge therefrom to the study of theoretical reason. Accordingly, my first three chapters are about practical reasoning, and it is only after them that I turn to examine how to adapt that account to theoretical reasoning and to reasoning to intention.

0.2 The Title of This Book

The subtitle of this book is 'A Theory of Practical Reasoning', but the title is 'Practical Shape'. What do I have in mind? The notion of practical shape, which is intended to be intriguing, and which I first introduced in *Moral Reasons* (ch. 7.2), is easy to confuse with another, namely that of the shape of practical thought. In talking about practical shape, I mean to be talking about the shape of the situation that confronts us, not about the shape of our thinking about that situation. Or rather, to the extent that our thinking has a shape, it is an attempt to capture in the mind a shape that the situation has independently of whether we recognize it or not. And that shape is practical, since it consists in a configuration of considerations relevant to one's choice of action.

First, then, how can a collection of considerations relevant to action be said to have a shape? Well, consider the idea that the only things relevant to how to act are the reasons for and against acting. The task of reasoning is to add up the reasons against and the reasons in favour, and to decide which are the weightier. (Benjamin Franklin seems to have thought that the only question is which are the more numerous.) On this picture of the elements of the situation that are relevant to action, I would say that there is little mileage in any idea of a practical shape. It is just two blobs, one on each side, and the question is which is the bigger blob. The metaphor of weighing is eminently suited to this conception, and for that reason is suspect if it is intended to do all the work; I happily allow that we can make a comparative assessment of the strengths of reasons, and that this can be thought of as weighing, but want to insist that much of the interesting work is done before we get to that stage. So I will be suggesting that the various aspects of the situation that confronts us relate to each other in a variety of interesting ways, each relevant to the question how to act and so to the eventual outcome, and that the aim of practical reasoning is to capture the relevances of all the differently relevant features, in the attempt to determine which course (or courses) of action is (or are) best suited to the demands of the situation. When I say 'relevances', this is because, while some considerations will indeed function as separate reasons, others will be doing other jobs, some of which have received quite a lot of attention in recent philosophical discussions of reasons. It is the presence of various differently relevant considerations that gives the situation its practical shape, as I call it, and it is the task of judgement to determine that shape as best it can. We are trying to get it right, and getting it right means conceiving of the situation as in fact it is, in all its glorious complexity. So there is a shape to the situation and we are trying to get our thought to fit that shape. The shape of the thinking is intended to match the shape of the situation.

This is a brand of normative realism. The notion of shape is a normative one, since the shape of the situation consists in the ways in which the various aspects of it combine to call for one form of response rather than any other. (They don't always do this, of course, since sometimes we have two equally good options—but sometimes not.) The shape of our thought is simply the way we shape the situation up, but the situation has a shape of its own, which we are trying to get our thought to fit. So when my editor (influenced by one of the readers for OUP) suggested that my title should be *The Shape of Practical Reasoning*, this showed to me that I had failed to bring out the normative realism implicit in my whole approach.

0.3 The Primacy of the Practical

In the first section of this Introduction I claimed that reasoning is reasoning, wherever we find it, but that we do better to start by thinking about practical reasoning, since those who work in the other direction have tended to make mistakes about theoretical reasoning, which they then impose on the practical side with the result that what I think of as practical reasoning—namely, reasoning to action—becomes incomprehensible. In this very weak sense, then, I have already suggested that the practical should be tackled first, and to that extent is primary.

But there is another sense in which we might think of a Primacy of the Practical, which emerges at various points in what is to follow. The clearest case of this comes when we think about reasons to intend to act in various ways. Suppose that I have decided to repay the money at the end of the week; so now this is what I intend to do. I presumably have reasons for that intention. Many of these reasons are also reasons to pay the money back by then. The question then arises which way round it goes, if either: are they reasons to intend (or to have decided) to pay it back by then because they are reasons to pay it back by then, or are they reasons to pay it back by then because they are reasons to intend to pay it back by then, or are the two sorts of reasons simply independent? To me it seems just obvious that they are reasons to intend to pay it back because they are reasons to pay it back. This is what I mean by the Primacy of the Practical. It concerns reasons in the first instance, rather than reasoning.

The question then arises how far this phenomenon reaches. Consider the moral case. Here we have a reason why one ought to pay it back by the end of the week; as I would say, there is a consideration which supports, or generates, a moral claim. But then that same consideration is probably a reason to pay the money back by then. Again we can ask: is that consideration a reason why one ought to pay it back because it is a reason to pay it back (and no doubt a reason of a certain sort), or does it work the other way round? I suggest that, normally at least, it works the other way around. A reason why one ought to F is normally that reason because it is a reason to F. The practical reason is also a moral reason, and it is the latter partly because it is the former. (Obviously something extra is needed to turn an ordinary practical reason into a moral one.) This is another example of the Primacy of the Practical.

The significance of this thesis, which as I have said is about reasons, is revealed when we consider the view that practical reasoning can only take us to conclusions about how we ought to act (or have most reason to act, or some other such conclusion), and never to acting itself, and the view that practical reasoning can only take us to intending to act in certain ways, never actually to acting in those ways. Though these views are both about reasoning rather than about reasons, I take them to be at odds with the Primacy of the Practical.

0.4 Minimalism and Focalism

Ray Buchanan helpfully suggested to me that my account of reasoning is a sort of minimalism. Instead of giving a detailed account of some form of reasoning, most probably theoretical reasoning or even instrumental reasoning, and then trying to show how other forms of reasoning resemble that sufficiently to count as reasoning too, what I say is that in reasoning one moves from considerations adduced, considerations of sufficient complexity for what is going on not just to be acting for (or more generally responding to) a reason, to whatever sort of response is (as we take it) most favoured by those considerations, taken together. I then urge that the various dimensions of complexity, as they emerge, do not vary significantly across different forms of reasoning; that is, they are equally relevant whether we are reasoning to belief, to intention, or to action.

This is worth counting as minimalism because the detailed accounts of different forms of reasoning, say formally valid reasoning, on one side, and instrumental reasoning, on another (and these two are indeed very different from one another), are written on top of a more general sameness which can get obscured if one is over-impressed with the differences that are certainly there. In particular, one can get over-excited about the nature of reasoning to a necessary means, and find oneself writing a general account of instrumental reasoning which rules out reasoning to a sufficient means altogether. Minimalism warns, or urges, us not to be over-impressed by any particular form of reasoning in that way. The sameness consists in the fact that reasoning consists in an attempt to determine what sort of response is most favoured by the considerations at issue, and responding in that way if one can. That is effectively a matter of *form*. We add *matter* to that form (and I do this in Chapter 3) when we give the non-formal relations between different considerations which are relevant in their different ways to the strength of the case that is made. An account of those relations would amount to a substantial, or material, theory of practical relevance.

Now many theorists suppose that any *formal* enquiry into the nature of practical reasoning is aiming at providing necessary and sufficient conditions for reasoning of that sort to occur. It would follow directly from this that since someone may reason practically and fail to act accordingly, practical reasoning does not itself include the performance of the relevant action. And (though this is not so often noticed) since someone may reason theoretically and fail to form the relevant belief as a result, theoretical reasoning cannot itself include any resulting belief.

But my purpose is not that of providing necessary and sufficient conditions for practical or for theoretical reasoning. It is rather to come to an understanding of practical reasoning by giving an account of certain instances, carefully chosen for the purpose, and offering to understand other putative cases in the light of those. I think of this as a *focalist* programme. That programme amounts to saying: these things are practical reasoning, and anything sufficiently relevantly similar to them is practical reasoning too. Similarly, but more generally, we can say that these things are reasoning and anything sufficiently similar to them is reasoning too. This enables us to escape the problems that troubled Paul Grice so much in the early pages of his *Aspects of Reason* (2001). He wanted to know how we could contrive to count bad reasoning as reasoning without being thereby forced to allow any rubbishy passage of thought to count as reasoning. The answer to this is simply to say that those rubbishy passages of thought are not sufficiently similar to the good cases. Focalism also enables us to avoid objections that derive from the fact that some instances of practical reasoning are not completed, in the sense that the relevant action does not occur for one reason or another. (Death would be such a reason.) Since these are indeed instances of reasoning, even if incomplete, one is tempted to infer that action is extraneous to any process of reasoning. I resist that inference, as will become most clear in Chapter 8.

Instances of focalism can be found elsewhere in philosophy. They tend to involve three moves. First, we identify certain cases as focal. Second, we determine a similarity relation between the focal cases and any peripheral cases. Third, we identify a dependence relation that holds between the focal and the peripheral cases.[1]

My own brand of focalism, or at least the sort of focalism I think of as instantiated in my approach to practical reasoning, is slightly less demanding that this. I am, as I said, not looking for necessary and sufficient conditions of anything. I give an account of certain successful cases of practical reasoning, and identify other processes as reasoning, or as practical reasoning, to the extent that they are relevantly similar to my focal cases.

0.5 The Structure of This Book

The book proceeds as follows. First I lay out, as best I can, a range of considerations that have led people to be so certain that reasoning cannot lead to action in the way that it can lead to belief. I do this, partly to show that I am aware of these considerations, and partly so that we can be sure that, to the extent that there is justice in them, the account I will be offering can accommodate them. In Chapter 2 I give the argument that first led me to the views I here propound, which is based on the simple question whether action can stand to the considerations in the light of which we act in the same sorts of relation that a belief can stand to the considerations in the light of which we adopt it. My answer to this question is yes; but it takes two chapters for the details of that answer to emerge. Then what I have to do is to tackle what one might call an inferential understanding of theoretical reasoning, which I do in Chapter 4. Since there can be no analogous inferential understanding of practical reasoning, I need to offer an account of theoretical reasoning

---

[1] In these remarks I owe much to discussion with Daniel Wodak.

that can, if not replace the inferential account, exactly, still underpin and explain whatever justice there is in it. My aim is to show that theoretical and practical reasoning are in all essentials pretty much indistinguishable from each other.

Chapter 5 is on moral reasoning. Moral reasoning seems to stand between practical reasoning and theoretical reasoning, since it seems to be reasoning to a belief but is also about what to do. What is more, many suppose that reasoning to the rightness of a particular way of acting is necessarily inferential, since it involves subsumption under a moral principle. Those who know my work on particularism in ethics will not be surprised to find that I reject that supposition. I do not entirely reject the idea that moral reasoning is reasoning to belief, for after all there is such a process as determining, by reason, that a proposed course of action would be wrong. But I also allow that someone can be said to be reasoning morally if they reason as a moral person would, without needing therefore to reach an explicitly moral conclusion along the way. It is enough if they consider the various morally relevant considerations and come thereby to act in the way those considerations recommend, taken as a whole. Such a person would be reasoning morally even if the concepts of right and wrong, ought and ought not, do not appear explicitly in the passage of their thought.

Chapter 6 stands back from the details that have emerged so far and looks more generally at the picture that has resulted. In particular, it is concerned with the hope that we might minimize such differences as have emerged between theoretical and practical reasoning. My general picture of reasoning sees it as a process in which we work from a detailed conception of the situation that confronts us to a response that is of the sort most favoured by the relevant considerations, taken as a whole. That response will be action (in practical reasoning) or belief (in theoretical reasoning). The difference between the two forms of reasoning lies in the way we explain the relevant favouring relations. Practical favouring is explained by appeal to values, but theoretical favouring is explained by probability of truth (broadly speaking). Chapter 6 looks at ways of reducing this last contrast, mainly that of accepting that truth is a value.

Chapter 7 is on instrumental reasoning, which many have thought to be the only form that practical reasoning can take. Some even restrict it further than that, to instrumental reasoning to a necessary means. I resist that view, and also reject the picture of practical reasoning that generates it. The resources that I used in my accounts of practical reasoning more generally, and of theoretical reasoning, prove quite sufficient to deal with all the various forms that instrumental reasoning can take. Some alternative forms are: reasoning to a sufficient means, and reasoning to a contributory or partial means which is neither sufficient nor necessary. These topics reappear in Chapter 9.

Finally, in Chapters 8 and 9 I try to tackle the two main forms of serious opposition to my account of practical reasoning, which I associate mainly with Joseph Raz and John Broome. Their views are well worked out, and entirely different from the largely implicit objections that I consider in Chapter 1. Chapter 10 attempts to tie up some loose ends, and to place my views in the context of those of others.

1

What Is the (Supposed) Problem about Practical Reasoning?

In this chapter I lay out various considerations that have persuaded people, or that might have influenced people to believe, that reasoning cannot 'conclude in' action in the way that it can 'conclude in' belief.

I reserve for Chapters 8 and 9 the discussion of two views about the impossibility of practical reasoning which I take much more seriously.

1.1 Acting in the Light of Reasoning vs Acting for a Reason

I start by distinguishing acting for a reason from acting in the light of reasoning. Whenever we act in the light of reasoning, there will be some reason for which we act—a reason which the reasoning will have located. But many simple cases of acting for a reason are not preceded by anything worth calling reasoning at all. If I get off the bus when my stop comes, normally I do this without thinking much; I get off the bus for a reason, certainly, that reason being that this is my stop. But I do not normally deliberate about the matter. I could do so—and would if, say, it occurs to me to stay on the bus till the next stop so as to buy something in a nearby shop. Perhaps it is raining, but I need the thing I am thinking of buying, but I am short of time because I have some friends coming round soon to pick up a bike. I mull this over for a while and decide to do without the thing I could have bought, which at least means that I will stay reasonably dry and be home in time for my friends. Simple acting for a reason, or acting for a simple reason, is not like that.

This book is not about acting for a reason. It is about acting in the light of reasoning. The difference lies in the complexity of what one is responding to. Certainly, no account of the relation between reasoning and action is possible without some prior account of what it is to act for a reason, and the relation between these two things will be important in what follows. But I do not have much that is especially new to say about reasons; my focus is on reasoning. And the phrase 'in the light of', which I use here and in many other places, is not supposed itself to mark the difference between actions that are responses to a reason and those that are responses to reasoning. One can act in the light of a reason.

So in reasoning I decide what to do in the light of various considerations, which may be competing or may simply combine in various ways to make a case for action. Some reasonings lead us from beliefs we have already to new beliefs—beliefs we didn't have before, but which we form in the light of our existing beliefs and our reasoning from those. Other reasonings take us from beliefs to intention (or from one intention to another). Yet other reasonings, we might think, take us from beliefs to action; in such cases our response to the beliefs to which we appeal consists in acting accordingly, not in forming some new belief. This book is about the latter sort of reasoning—if it exists at all. Many perfectly respectable thinkers hold that it doesn't. Everyone admits that people reason and then act in the light of their reasoning. So much is uncontentious. What is contentious is whether action can stand in much the same relation to the reasoning that precedes it as does belief, or whether, to get to the action, we have to pass through a new belief which is the 'real' product of the reasoning.

1.2 Two Lines of Attack

So one opinion is that our reasoning can indeed 'lead' us to action, but it can only do so by taking us first to a new belief; the reasoning takes us *first* or *immediately* to a new, intermediate belief, and only *second* or *mediately* to the action. The intermediate belief will be a belief that one ought to act in such and such a way, or that it would be best so to act, or that one has most reason to act in that way—something along those lines. Such beliefs are as far as reasoning can take us directly, and then of course we normally act accordingly—but that is a separate matter and nothing directly to do with the reasoning.

On this picture, there is no genuinely *practical* reasoning in the sense I give to that phrase. The most we could claim is that some reasoning will be practically relevant, in that its outcome, its conclusion, consists in a determination of how we are to (or ought to) act. But the answer to the question how we are to act is never itself an action; it is always a belief—a belief to the effect that this is how we should act, or is what we should do, or is the thing to do, or would be best. The role of reasoning, then, is always to take us from belief to belief, though some beliefs have a more direct relevance to practical decision than do others.

Another opinion, which we will confront directly in Chapter 9, is that reasoning can take us from a combination of intentions and beliefs to the formation of a derived intention. The standard example of this is reasoning to a necessary means. I intend to achieve a certain end, I recognize (believe) that if I don't act in a certain way, I will fail to achieve that end, and so I form the intention to act in that way. Of course I may eventually actually act in that way, but the action lies beyond the scope of any reasoning. So here again there is going to be no genuinely practical reasoning; the most we get is what we might call (to coin a phrase) intentional reasoning.

1.3 Aristotle's Picture

Aristotle, however, is standardly translated as writing in his *Nicomachaean Ethics* that 'whenever some one thing is derived from them [a pair of premises, one universal and one particular], that conclusion must in the one case be asserted by the soul, and in the case of practical reasoning immediately be done; e.g. if everything sweet should be tasted, and this is sweet (which is one of the particular premises), the agent who is able and is not held back must simultaneously actually do this' (EN 7.3, 1147a26–31 (my translation)).

This remark of Aristotle's has reverberated down the centuries, but more recently few have been found to defend it. The idea that the conclusion of reasoning, of this or any other form, can be an action has seemed to many, perhaps even to most, to be quite unsustainable. The main purpose of this book, however, is to show a way in which Aristotle was right.

Of course I don't mean by this that I am going to defend all of the various things that Aristotle says on the topic. For instance, I don't think that the agent who has her premises lined up in the right way *must* act in the way those premises go to recommend. And I don't think Aristotle was right to cast all practical reasoning in syllogistic form (just as it would not be right to cast all theoretical reasoning in syllogistic form). This second mistake is understandable in someone who 'discovered' that form, but is not, in my view, the way to go. It is the first example of several that we will meet along the way, of someone who understands practical reasoning in terms derived from thinking about theoretical reasoning. (Anthony Price makes a similar criticism in his book *Virtue and Reason in Plato and Aristotle*.)

But my intention is to produce an account of the matter under which Aristotle's basic claim that theoretical and practical reasoning are fundamentally very similar turns out to be correct. There are differences between them, yes, but those differences are not a matter of basic structure. They lie elsewhere. The views of Aristotle's critics derive either from a mistaken conception of theoretical reasoning, at one end, or from a mistaken conception of action at the other.

I have to admit, however, that there are lots of *apparent* reasons for siding with the critics and against Aristotle. In what follows I try to bring out what I think of as those considerations that have, either explicitly or implicitly, mainly influenced those critics. But don't forget, while reading these, that I think that in one way or another they are all mistakes.

1.4 Can the Conclusion Be an Action?

I have already suggested that in considering the nature of practical reasoning one has to recognize that a certain picture of theoretical reasoning (that is, of reasoning from beliefs to belief) is often lying in the background—a picture that already makes the likelihood of there being genuinely practical reasoning seem very small. One apparent feature of theoretical reasoning is that one can write it down. One can write down the premises and one can write down the conclusion. And one certainly could not do that if the conclusion were an action, because one cannot write an action down. So when one sees on the page something like:

A man in my situation needs a beer and that is a beer
So:

It is very hard to get the drinking that is supposed to be the conclusion down on the page.[1] If we try something like:

A man in my situation needs a beer, and that is a beer
So: I drink that beer

we get something literally unintelligible, since 'I drink that beer' means nothing as it stands; for instance, it does not mean that I am drinking that beer. And whatever it might mean, one might say, it cannot actually *be* my drinking that beer. If we had written:

A man in my situation needs a beer, and that is a beer
So: I am drinking that beer

We would have something intelligible, something that can be written down, but still pretty silly. And if we put instead:

A man in my situation needs a beer, and that is a beer
So: I will drink that beer.

we have again something intelligible, and maybe the conclusion is even true, but what the reasoning takes us to is not my drinking that beer, but that I will drink it, which looks a lot more like something to be believed than like an action, something done or to be done. Kenny speaks for many (though not for me) when he writes: 'Whatever be the sense of this passage of Aristotle,[2] the correct account seems to be that the conclusion of a piece of practical reasoning is a description of an action to be done: a fiat concerning the reasoner's action' (1975: 98). And surely we have to allow that no description of an action, not even a description of an action-to-be-done, can be identified with the action it describes.

So we already have something that looks like a difficulty. Reasoning can only take us to conclusions that can be 'asserted by the soul'; it

---

[1] It is very hard to make this point reasonably succinctly while still respecting my original distinction between acting for a reason, which seems to be really what is going on in the example in the text above, and acting in the light of reasoning. To respect that distinction I would need to provide examples that involve a more complex train of thought than this simple one presents. But for the sake of the point I am trying to make, the distinction between simplicity and complexity is not really relevant; so I ask the reader's indulgence for the way in which I have cut certain corners here.

[2] Kenny is here referring to Aristotle's *De Motu Animalium* 7017a7ff.

cannot take us to actions. Another similar problem revolves around the notion of a conclusion. Where there is reasoning, we think, there must be premises and a conclusion. So we have some premises, that a man in my situation needs a beer and that that is a beer. What is the conclusion? Well, the person drawing the conclusion is me, and what is it that I conclude? Again we have various choices and none of them seems very convincing. I could conclude that I drink that beer (which is meaningless), that I am drinking it (in which case the reasoning is already too late), or that I will drink it (which is not an action but a prediction, something to be believed and perhaps acted on, but still not the drinking) or that I should drink it. In fact, it seems plain that what one concludes cannot be an action. (Though of course in the sense of 'finish' one can conclude an action, as when one concludes one's opening speech with a nice compliment for one's host.) So, it seems, the conclusion of practical reasoning cannot be an action. And similarly, one might think, there cannot be premises for an action either.

A further difficulty comes from the connection between belief and action that there would have to be if one could somehow derive the action from the beliefs. In theoretical reasoning we derive one belief from some others. So we face again the question how one could possibly *derive* an action from beliefs in that sort of way. The term we use to mark the derivation is 'so'. I used it in that role for the examples above. And we understand perfectly well the 'so' that links premises to conclusion. It is the 'so' of 'so it is true that . . .' or of 'so it is probably true that . . .'. But what would be the sense of a practical 'so'? It must be something other than the 'so' involved in 'so I am drinking' or in 'so I will drink'; and 'so I drink' is meaningless. It is as meaningless as 'so he drinks'.

Or is it? Notice the sense of 'he was thirsty, and so he drank a beer'. Maybe there is a practical 'so' to be unearthed. If so, it will not have the sense of 'so it is (probably) true that he drank a beer'. What sense could it have, then? Perhaps the practical 'so' means something more like 'for that reason'. Note also the possibility of 'he is thirsty and so he drinks a beer'.

1.5 Building Grids

I have not finished mentioning putative difficulties. Another derives from a certain way of thinking about reasoning. We have to distinguish between the activity of reasoning and those aspects of that activity that can be written down on the page. Consider this grid (the first of many):

Belief	p
Belief	q
Belief	r

This is an attempt to map an ordinary piece of theoretical reasoning. An example might be a detective reasoning from two pieces of evidence, perhaps that the husband had a strong motive (p) and that he gave a false alibi (q), to the conclusion that the husband is the guilty person (r). Reasoning of this sort has no visible structure in the right-hand column. Things would be different if we had a case like this:

Belief	p
Belief	If p then q
Belief	q

This grid is an attempt to map a simple instance of reasoning using *modus ponens*. There is a reasoner who has two beliefs, that p and that if p then q, and who reasons from what she believes to the conclusion that q, which she adopts.

In addition to the considerations that appear in the right-hand column of these two grids, the first two of which are the things from which she reasons, the grids above also have a place for the relevant psychological attitudes in the reasoner. We are, after all, trying to map an occurrent passage of theoretical reasoning, in which the reasoner is reasoning from things she believes to something else which she comes to believe. So we need to map the reasoner's side of things as well as the logical structure (if any) of her beliefs taken together. We have given the latter by displaying what she believes as separate from her believing of it.[3] After all, it wouldn't work at all if the reasoner did not believe that p, but, say,

---

[3] For this reason the grids I offer are not in accordance with the influential views of G. Harman. Harman wanted to separate a structure of believings, with their content, or things believed, from logical structures that exemplify properties such as validity. One

doubted whether *p*. We might try to represent a case that starts from a doubt like this:

Doubt	*p*
Belief	If *q* then *p*
Doubt	*q*

But I suspect that this would be unwise. How can I reason from *p* if I doubt that *p*? And I am not reasoning from my doubt; if I were, my first premise would be 'I doubt that *p*' (and I would have to believe this), and as we will see in 7.6–7, these autobiographical premises introduce all sorts of difficulties. An alternative is to say that someone who doubts whether *p* has a reason to doubt whether *q*, given him by the fact that (as he supposes) *q* implies *p*. Or we might think of our doubting reasoner as reasoning from something he believes, namely that it is doubtful whether *p*. I will consider these deviant or special cases of reasoning in more detail in 7.9.

So in each grid the psychological attitudes of the reasoner are broken up into, on the left, the type of mental state or attitude at issue, and on the right, that to which the reasoner has that attitude. So since we are mainly dealing with belief, it is believing on the left and the thing believed on the right, and theoretical reasoning is the passage from certain believings, where the things believed are acting as premises, to another believing.

One minor criticism of such grids is that they fail to express the direction, or flow, of the reasoning. But I don't know how to represent that in a grid. Remembering that there is a direction in the process as well as in the structure, one could try this:

Belief	*p*
Belief	If *p* then *q*
So: Belief	So: *q*

reason for doing this was that normative constraints on believings are grounded in other believings. This is not something that I would accept, for reasons given in the Appendix to Chapter 4.

But this isn't very convincing as it stands; there seems to be one too many 'so's. But it is not clear which one to keep and which one to leave out.

1.6 Finding a Place for Action

Leaving that issue aside, let us work with the idea that grids like these can be used to capture significant aspects of theoretical reasoning, the passage from beliefs to belief. If so, there is a problem with the use of such grids to express practical reasoning, which is that one cannot fill in the bottom line. Consider the next two grids:

Belief	A man like me needs a beer
Belief	This is a beer
So: drinking	

and

Belief	A man like me needs a beer
Belief	This is a beer
	So: drinking

We have to put the action on one side or the other, but neither side seems right. What is more, if it appears on only one side, we cannot represent the reasoning in any way analogous to what seems to be a perfectly satisfactory way of representing theoretical reasoning. And this is because with belief we can distinguish between the believing, mapped on the left, and the thing believed, mapped on the right. We know there are differences between these things because the believing may be incautious, but the thing believed cannot be either cautious or incautious. Again, the believing may be responsible, but the thing believed cannot be. The thing believed can be surprising without the believing of it being so, and vice versa.

But now try to run a similar distinction between the doing and what is done. It is much harder to persuade oneself that the thing done is distinct in the right sort of way from the doing of it. A thing achieved is distinct from the achieving of it, and a product is distinct from the producing of it (from the productive process, that is). But what is done does not seem to be distinct from the doing of it. To check on this, ask yourself what properties the doing might have that the thing done does not have. If the doing took a long time, the thing done took a long time. If the thing done was stupid, so was the doing of it. And so on.

Could we then try to break the action up in a rather different way, into a bodily movement and an intentional 'component'? For the moment all I will say about this suggestion is that it would do little to rehabilitate the notion of practical reasoning in those whose model for reasoning is, as the grids have it, one that operates on a distinction between a mental state on the left and something like the content of that state on the right. What we would have on the left, a mere motion, seems incapable of having any sort of intentional content. It might be accompanied, or caused by, some sort of purposing, but this is an entirely different relation from that between a belief and what is believed.

A different way of carving the action up so as to have something to put on either side on the bottom line would be to distinguish the mental aspect of the action, understood as an intention, from the physical aspect, the movement. But this attempt to extract the intentionality of the action from the movement leaves a remainder that is a mere motion, that is, a change in place or shape. But no such thing fits well at the bottom of the right-hand column.

So here is another reason why we might feel that reasoning cannot take us from belief to action. There are real difficulties in locating an action on the sort of grid we can supposedly use to map theoretical reasoning. Of course my main point is going to be that even if we cannot locate action on our grid, this does nothing to show that there cannot be such a thing as practical reasoning. In the present discussion I am merely running through considerations that might persuade one that genuine practical reasoning is impossible. So though I recognize that there are difficulties in capturing practical reasoning on this sort of grid, the underlying point will be that it does not really matter whether that is so or not. Nothing has been said to show that an approach in terms of grids is compulsory.

1.7   Drawing the Conclusion

There are also issues to do with the notion of a conclusion. Conclusions are drawn or reached, and the drawing of a conclusion might perhaps be viewed as the beginning or onset of the relevant belief, or (perhaps better) as causing oneself to have that belief. The conclusion itself is what one comes to believe when one draws that conclusion. So there is the act of concluding that q, and there is the thing concluded, that q. The act of concluding does not appear on our grid, but the result of that act is that one now believes that q. The act of concluding must happen at some time, presumably the time at which one comes to believe. All this, one would have thought, is quite harmless.

But it is not harmless as far as reasoning to an action is concerned. For the question will be when the conclusion was drawn. Actions take time, in a way that 'coming to believe' or 'causing oneself to believe' does not—even if those are actions too. So: is our practical conclusion drawn as the action starts, all the way through the action somehow, or only when the action is finally done and dusted? No one of these answers seems appropriate, and that makes the question seem misconceived. One feels that the need to answer it is fictitious. But it would not be fictitious if there were such a thing as reasoning to action, conceived on the model of reasoning to belief.

We might try to avoid this sort of worry by thinking that we draw the practical conclusion when we decide to act, just as we draw the theoretical conclusion when we decide to accept that p. But this seems simply to abandon the idea that it is the action that is the conclusion, in favour of the idea that the practical conclusion is a decision. (Admittedly, to decide is to act; but the idea that all practical reasoning ends in decision was not what Aristotle had in mind; he was thinking of eating chicken (in one example), not of deciding to eat chicken either now or later.) And anyway, sometimes acting is the form that deciding takes. (What shall I do? This!)

1.8   Belief and Action

The supposed difficulties raised in the previous sections all stem from a certain model of theoretical reasoning—one that seems to leave little room for practical reasoning, reasoning to action. But there are other difficulties that stem from the differences between belief and reasoning, on one side, and action on the other. It is very tempting to think that there is more of a gap between thought and action than there is between thought and thought, so that reasoning that takes us from thought to thought is easier to conceive than is reasoning that takes us from thought to action.

Reasoning is a mental process, and action is (mostly) physical. One might wonder how a physical event or process could be the conclusion of a mental one. In particular, one might wonder how a passage of thought could be concluded by a physical event. It could be stopped by one, of course; but the conclusion of reasoning is not the same thing as what causes the reasoning to stop. Death will stop reasoning pretty effectively, but one's death could hardly be the conclusion of anything except of one's life. And a passage of thought could be naturally followed by a physical event, I suppose—by blushing, for instance. But if one is wanting to see the physical event as standing in the same relation to the preceding mental process as does some appropriate mental event, it looks as if one is going to have a hard time.

The answer to this is that an action is not a merely physical event. There is a difference between my body's moving and my moving my body. My moving my body consists in my causing my body to move, and the motion that I cause is not the action of causing that motion. (Here the phrase 'causing my body to move' is not to be understood as 'causing my body to move itself' but simply as 'causing motions of my body'; the only agent here is me.) So the motion of the body is a physical event, but this does not mean that the causing of that motion is a physical event. Indeed, it is not even clear that causings are events at all. For causal relations between events are not further events inserted between the cause-event and the effect-event. So we should be wary of taking it for granted that the causal relation between an agent and a bodily motion, the causing, is an event.

Here I simply assert, without argument, the conception of action that at the moment of writing seems to me to be most fruitful: to act is to cause a change. To defend that conception properly would take a whole book in itself—and that book has not yet been written. The main recent sources for the general idea are Alvarez and Hyman (1998) and Lowe (2008). Prichard does remark in his 'Does Moral Philosophy Rest on a Mistake?' that 'we...mean by an action merely the conscious origination of something' (2002: 12), but here he must be talking only of intentional action. However, what is important for me is not that this particular conception of action be correct, but that certain other conceptions (especially that of an action as a bodily motion caused by mental states) be incorrect. There is an alternative, post-Aristotelian conception of an action as the realization of a potential in the agent, under which one's arm's rising can be identical with one's raising one's arm. (For this conception, see Coope 2007.) Here I do not want to adjudicate between the Aristotelian conception and the one I presently favour. I am happy to adopt whichever turns out eventually to be the more defensible; either will be perfectly suitable to my purposes in this book.

This distinction between my moving my body, which is a causing, and the motion of my body, which is what is caused (or, perhaps better, is the result of my causing) makes one wonder how to understand an unintended sneeze. Is such a sneeze an action of mine or just something that happens to me? The latter seems the better option, but if so, such sneezes cannot be the conclusion of practical reasoning. For if any actions at all can be conclusions of practical reasoning, only intentional actions can play this role. Things done by mistake, by accident, inadvertently or unintentionally cannot play this role. They may come after reasoning, but cannot play the special role of being a conclusion of that reasoning. Involuntary actions are different, because they can be intended (Hyman 2015: 4.5) and can be the product of reasoning, as when one yields to a threat. The issue, then, is not so much about action in general as about intentional action.

I understand an intentional action, the sort of action that can conclude reasoning, as one that is informed by an understanding of what one is doing, of the change one is causing; and this relation of 'being informed' is not to be taken merely as that of being accompanied by mental comment or preceded by mental cause. The 'mentality', or mindedness, of intentional action is essential, not incidental, to it, and lasts as long as the action does. In this way we can generate what one might think of as a content for an action; only intentional actions have such a content. It is in virtue of having such a content that the action can have the sort of appropriateness to the situation that is involved when the action is done in the light of the various considerations adduced. One can only act in such a light when one has some conception of what one is doing, a conception that informs and shapes one's response as it unfolds.

This conception of intentional action is not enough alone to make sense of the possibility of practical reasoning. The question will be: if there is both practical and theoretical reasoning, what is the common feature that makes them both reasoning?

1.9 Inference, Premise, and Conclusion

There are further difficulties, which are to do with the notion of inference. Crudely put, it seems possible to infer a proposition, and even to infer a belief, but the idea of inferring an action sounds incoherent. Can one infer drinking, infer a drinking, or infer to drink? It also seems impossible to infer an emotion; but we should not take that as a reason to deny that emotions can be the proper product of reasoning. (We might, of course, wish to deny it for other reasons.)

More cautiously, we could say that there are two respectable notions of inference, despite its prevalence in the work of von Wright (1963, 1972) and Anscombe (1974). One is inference as action, the doing of something; the action done will be that of passing from beliefs to belief in a certain way, perhaps. The other notion is the idea of an inferential relation between certain sentences, or between certain propositions. The relation at issue will be the one that makes the action of inferring appropriate, permitted, or required. As we might say, 'there is an inference to be drawn here'. If we are dealing with a formally valid deductive inference, that relation between the relevant sentences or propositions will be a formal one, to do with the form rather than the matter of the inference concerned. The truth of the premises guarantees the truth of the conclusion because of formal relations between the relevant sentences/propositions. If the inference is deductive but not formal, as in the inference from 'that is a vixen' to 'that is an animal', the explanation of the permissibility of inferring the latter from the former will have to appeal to something other than form. (It is not as if the inference is really from 'that is a female fox and an animal' to 'that is an animal'; nor is it from 'that is a female fox and all female foxes are animals' to 'that is an animal'.) And there are other possibilities as well, of course, as when we come to probabilistic inference.

However, all this can be easily mapped on our grid. The notion of inference as action is to be found in the left-hand column, in the move from beliefs already formed to a new belief; the notion of inference as a relation between propositions is to be found in the right-hand column. Of course one does not exactly find either of those things explicitly presented in the grid; but what is explicitly presented there is the material we need for the two notions of inference. The rather dubious grid that contained two notions of 'so', one in the left column and one in the right, is the one that comes nearest to showing this. And as we have already seen, there is just no room for any action on that grid other than the action of inferring.

So it seems that there are problems with the idea of inferring an action, problems with the idea that an action can be the conclusion of an inference, and problems with the idea that there can be premises for an action. I think of these three difficulties as different aspects of one and the same difficulty. The three notions of premise, conclusion, and inference make a family. If there is inference, it must be from premises to a conclusion. If there is a conclusion, it must be the conclusion of inference from premises, and if there are premises, they must be premises for a potential inference to a conclusion.

The solution to this family of issues is to abandon talk of practical inference altogether. Practical reasoning, if there is to be such a thing, is not going to be any form of inference, and it will have neither premises nor conclusion. It is true that one reasons from something to something else—from the considerations adduced to the action done in their light, as I am going to say. One adduces various considerations, considers their interrelations, and acts in the light of that. But officially I now abandon any attempt to show how or that an action could be the conclusion of an inference.

1.10 The Grids

I should strike a note or two of warning about the grids that I have been using. I introduced these initially in order to make a point that may have influenced the thinking of some who take the view that one cannot reason to action. That point was that action cannot appear on the grid. In response to that point, one could ask why we should expect all reasoning to be capable of being represented in a grid of that sort. But I did not ask that question. I did not challenge the use of grids at all.

One important and I hope obvious point is that the grid represents a process, not a steady state. A deliberator adduces considerations one after another, and comes to act (or believe or intend) accordingly. So there is a temporal order from top to bottom. Of course it is not vital that the process should have had this rather than that order, and often actual cases of reasoning are pretty much of a jumble anyway. My use of the grids as an artificial representational device should not be taken to imply otherwise.

But these grids do introduce various potentially dubious assumptions which could usefully be brought to light. Let me make this point with respect to reasoning to belief.

The first assumption is that everything present in the right-hand column, except for what is on the bottom line, counts as part of the case for believing the 'conclusion'. But often we reach our conclusion despite various counter-indications, which play a role in our reasoning even though they are eventually to be put aside. In a more realistic representation of, say, a detective's reasoning, we have to find room for things that are not themselves part of the case for believing the conclusion.

The second assumption is more general: it is that everything on the right-hand side is doing the same sort of job. Each is a premise. But I will be arguing in the next two chapters that there are many different ways in which considerations can contribute to a case for belief (or for action, come to that).

The third assumption (less forceful, I think, than the previous two) is that one can only reason from things that one believes. If there is truth in this, it will have to be compatible with the fact that there does at least *seem* to be room for reasoning from doubt, hope, and fear. To take hope: I hope that my daughter got home safely last night, I believe that she will only have done so if she managed to catch the last train, and so I hope that she caught the last train. The 'so' in this looks like exactly the same kind of 'so' as marks the acceptance of (i.e. belief in) a conclusion in the light of evidence. I discuss this sort of difficulty in 7.9.

Despite all these drawbacks, along with others to be raised later (see 3.1, 3.6, 4.1, and 7.9), I will continue to make some of my points with the help of grids. This is not because I am especially fond of grids—in fact, rather the opposite if anything—but because they offer me a perspicuous way of showing visually how I conceive of reasoning, whether practical or otherwise. All this is yet to come.

2

How Practical Reasoning
Is Possible

I have now done with raising difficulties. It is time to turn from
destruction to construction.

2.1 A Telling Question

The supposed difficulties we saw in Chapter 1 derived mainly from a
certain picture of theoretical reasoning. We said: theoretical reasoning is
to be understood in this way, and nothing worth calling practical reasoning could be understood in that way. This was, of course, nothing
specially to do with the deductive, indeed the formal, nature of some of
our examples. The points would have been just as good if we had been
reasoning from the previous behaviour of the buses to the probable time
of arrival of the next bus. All that mattered was that there were premises
and a conclusion, and the idea that no action can be related to premises in
that sort of way.

But now let us stop thinking about premises and conclusions for a
moment, and put aside our conceptions of theoretical reasoning. We
would get the smallest possible difference between theoretical reasoning
and practical reasoning if in the latter an action plays (or at least can
play) the role played by a belief, or the adoption of a belief, in the former.
So let us change our question to one that introduces as few preconceptions as possible. We might try this question:

Is it possible for an action that is a response to the considerations
adduced in deliberation, taken as a whole, to stand in the same relation
to those considerations as the relation in which belief stands, as a
response, to the considerations adduced in reasoning, taken as a whole?

The most important aspect of this question is that it treats both action and belief as responses—as ways in which we respond to considerations adduced in deliberation or reasoning. The question 'What am I to do here?' is treated as similar to the question 'What am I to think here?' This is a very important shift of focus.

But this question speaks of 'the same relation', and one might think that there might be several relations in which belief stands to the considerations adduced in reasoning. Nor can one really hope to avoid this difficulty by talking of the most telling relation, or something like that, because there might be no such 'most telling' relation. But we might ask instead what I will call the Question:

> To what extent is it possible for action that is a response to the considerations adduced in deliberation, to stand in the same relations to those considerations, taken as a whole, as those in which a belief that is a response to considerations adduced in reasoning stands to those considerations, taken as a whole?

My answer to this question is 'to a very considerable extent'—indeed, the match is almost perfect. Pretty much every relevant relation in which belief can stand to considerations adduced is one in which action can also stand. If I can make this response stick, I will have shown the respect in which Aristotle was right.

Note that the Question does not use the notions of premise, conclusion, or inference. The three members of this closed family of terms are to be avoided altogether, in order to minimize the effect of the admission that practical reasoning is not inference. We saw that the idea of inference is not friendly to Aristotle's picture, because the idea of inferring an action does not make good sense. Our Question is, as far as I can see, entirely clean so far as this goes. It is an open question, one that is in no danger of importing preconceptions before we have even got started. I confess that it does use a notion of deliberation, which we have not yet seen, and which it uses so as to get away from the notion of inference; and it uses the notion of a consideration, which is also new. But a consideration is meant to be just whatever it is that we start from, or with. It might be, for example, that there is beer in the fridge, that Socrates is a man, that we need a ride home—anything whatever that one can start from in deliberation or reasoning. And if there is any contrast between deliberation and reasoning, nothing is to hang on that. So let us use the term 'deliberation' for the process of weighing practical reasons, which is what its etymology would suggest, without intending any detailed account of how that process might be conceived: in particular, without supposing that it involves nothing else than this 'weighing', or even that in the end the metaphor of weighing will turn out to be appropriate. We could then leave the notion of reasoning to be used on the theoretical side, if we wanted, and simply ask whether the relations between the considerations adduced in (theoretical) reasoning and the belief that is our response to those considerations are significantly different from the relations between the considerations adduced in (practical) deliberation and the action that is our response to those considerations, or whether those relations might be the same. I stress again that, in this question, the phrase 'the belief that is our response' refers not to what we believe, but to our believing it. It is in believing this, or in doing that, that we respond to the considerations we adduce.

2.2 An Easy Answer

Now to this Question there seems to me to be an easy answer. To see that answer, let us first notice that the relation or relations we are interested in are mainly normative. Of course there are plenty of instances of unsound, or invalid, deliberation and reasoning. But for present purposes we are focusing on the good cases, where the relevant belief or action is supported by the considerations adduced, and adopted therefore. This notion of support is normative, as are other similar notions. There is, then, in these good cases, a normative relation between considerations and response. But this does not yet show, of course, that it is the same relation we are looking for on both sides.

Still, once we have got this far, it is easy to find the, or at least a same normative relation on both sides. The relation we are looking for is already perfectly familiar to those working in this sort of area. It is the famous, or infamous, favouring relation.[1] (I say 'infamous' only because I know that some people think that far too much has been made to hang

---

[1] Compare this suggestion with the suggestion made by Tenenbaum (2007), that good practical reasoning justifies its conclusion rather than guarantees the truth (or existence) of that conclusion. I am myself too wary of the notion of justification to use it in this way, and of course much good theoretical reasoning does not guarantee the truth of anything.

on this relation; for them, the present book will only make matters worse.) The considerations that are adduced in deliberation, and to which the relevant action is a response, are considerations that together favour that response, or favour responding in that way. The considerations adduced in reasoning to belief, and to which that belief is a response, are considerations that favour that response, or favour responding in that way. It is, as far as this goes, the same on both sides. So when an agent deliberates well and then acts accordingly, the action done is of the sort most favoured by the considerations rehearsed, taken as a whole—just as when an agent reasons well and then believes accordingly, the belief formed (the believing, that is, not the thing believed) is of the sort most favoured by the considerations rehearsed, again taken as a whole.[2]

So the 'same relations' of our question include centrally the favouring relation, and to that extent the answer to our question is easy. To the extent that the favouring relation is indeed central both to our account of deliberation leading to action and to our account of reasoning leading to belief, we may expect very considerable similarities between the two domains of reasoning. And what I will argue in the final sections of this chapter, and in the next, is that although there are other relations than the favouring relation that are relevant to the question what response to make to the situation that confronts us (whether our response is action or belief), still those further relations are all to be understood in terms of their relation to favouring. In that sense the favouring relation will be found to be central, and our easy answer to the Question will be secure.

I said above that the favouring relation is famous or infamous, and that it is infamous partly because some people think that far too much is made of it. But another source of infamy is that nobody has got near offering much of an account of that relation, or any sort of explication. It is not because the relation is unfamiliar; in fact it is almost too familiar. Features of our situation favour or call for certain responses. The relation involved is objective, there to be noticed. When we respond to considerations *as reasons*, we are tracking the favouring relation in which those considerations stand to a way of responding, or, as I tend to put it, acting in the light of those considerations. When we act in the light

---

[2] I leave for later (8.5) the question how to deal with cases where there are two equally good responses available to the agent, and the differences between that situation and the situation where two different beliefs are equally well supported by the evidence.

of considerations adduced in deliberation, again we are tracking the favouring relation in which those considerations, taken together, stand to acting as we do. There is of course a psychological aspect to this negotiation. Deliberation, or reasoning, is something we do, and can do consciously. Deliberation is our way of shaping up the situation that confronts us so as to reveal the course of action most favoured by the relevant considerations, taken together. There is a psychological aspect to this process, and an objective aspect. There is also a psychological aspect to the product, whether it be belief or action (see 1.8). But the relations that drive the reasoning, or the deliberation, are not themselves psychological. They are normative.

In discussion I have heard complaints (mainly from people whose first language is not English) that the favouring relation, far from being an objective normative relation between considerations and responses, is too anthropomorphic: that only people can favour things. I have a certain amount of sympathy with this worry; it first came to me from a Dutch audience, who said that the word in Dutch that best translates 'favour' applies to something that only people can do. To some extent such worries can be dispelled by reverting to the phrase 'count in favour of'. But if asked in turn what that means, it seems to me that we can only appeal to the distinction between 'for' and 'against'. And there is an anthropomorphic side even to that, because we can think that he is for it but she is against, and it is not obvious that considerations are capable of doing what we can do in this respect. A consideration that counts in favour of responding in a certain way is not in that sense 'for' that sort of response; it is not, as one might say, rooting for it. So there are problems here for those who would like to see some explication of the favouring relation. But this is not the place for further discussion of such issues. For present purposes, I propose to leave the infamousness of the favouring relation to one side and rely on its famousness.

But there are some other issues to do with the favouring relation that do require some discussion before we can move on, which the next few sections are intended to provide.

2.3 What Is Favoured: The Prichard Point

I said that in a successful case, the action done will be of the sort most favoured by the considerations adduced in reasoning, taken as a whole.

There is a difference between saying this and saying that the action done will be *the one* most favoured by the considerations adduced, and that difference is worth remarking at this early stage, so as to get it out into the open. (It will concern us more seriously later.) We owe to H. A. Prichard the point that a reason is never a reason for a particular act; it is and can only be a reason to act in a certain way. So the fact that I owe you £5 is a reason for me to pay you back when you ask for the money, but it is not a consideration that favours any particular way of paying you back; it leaves many aspects of that recommended reimbursement unspecified. As far as that reason is concerned, I can pay it back today or tomorrow, I can pay it back by cheque or in cash, I can pay it back graciously or churlishly, I can pay it back here rather than there—and so on. All that the reason does is to count in favour of my doing an action—some action or other—of the reimbursing sort.

I said that we owe this point to Prichard, but in fact the consideration that influenced Prichard was the fact that the reason is a reason for an action that has not yet been done, and so does not yet exist to be favoured by that reason. Worse: Prichard's own discussion was not about reasons, or even about rightness, but about obligations. What he actually wrote was this:

But, as we recognize when we reflect, there are no such characteristics of an action as ought-to-be-doneness and ought-not-to-be-doneness. This is obvious; for, since the existence of an obligation to do some action cannot possibly depend on actual performance of the action, the obligation itself cannot be a property which the action would have, if it were done.   (1932: 99)

Prichard wanted to destabilize a certain conception of moral decision in advance, when we decide to act but have not yet acted. We cannot suppose that an action that does not yet exist has somehow already got the property of being obligatory for us.[3] What we decide is *how* it would be right to act, or *how* we are obliged to act. This is not the same as a decision about some particular act, that this act is the obligatory one. It is

[3] Anscombe makes the same point, but about reasons (1957: 9). Michael Stocker writes: 'We fulfill duties by performing ... act tokens ... Nonetheless, it is not a duty to perform any act token. For we could have fulfilled the duty by doing another act token of the appropriate type. For example, even though that returning of the book fulfilled the promise to return the book, many other returnings of the book would have done so as well' (1968: 54). And Roderick Chisholm argues (wrongly, in my view) that the distinction between perfect and imperfect duties succumbs to the Prichard point (1980: fn. 6).

not as if all the available actions are there before us and that we select one as the one we ought to do. Since we are deciding in advance, there is no action there waiting to be chosen. Choosing actions is not like choosing a chocolate. When we make up our mind about our duty, then, all we can do is to fix on *a way* of acting. I decide that I ought to pay the money back; and this means, and can only mean, that I decide that whatever I do, one of my actions ought to be of the reimbursing sort. Some action I go on to do must be of that sort, though it will of course have many other properties about which the voice of duty is silent.

The relevance of all this is that even if we do allow ourselves to speak of a reason for an action, we should remember that no consideration favours a particular action somehow taken as a whole. All that a consideration can do is to favour acting in a certain way. So any suggestion that I may have made to the effect that 'the considerations that are adduced in deliberation, and to which the relevant action is a response, are considerations that favour that response', was incautious. (Perhaps I should now confess that it was deliberately so.) The proper way of putting it is this: 'when an agent deliberates well and then acts accordingly, the action done is *of the sort* most favoured by the considerations rehearsed, taken as a whole'. All that the reasons can do is to favour responding in a certain way—and there are many ways of responding in that way, as one might say.

But once we have realized the importance of the Prichard point, does it not serve to introduce a significant distinction between reasoning to action and reasoning to belief? Reasoning to action, I have now admitted, can take us only to 'acting in a certain way', and this falls short of taking us to a particular act. Any act of that sort will serve equally well. So the Prichard point seems to undermine any attempt to build an 'Aristotelian' view under which reasoning can take us to action in the way that it takes us to belief.

The question then is whether the Prichard point applies only to action, and not to belief. If so, a consideration is capable of favouring a particular belief but not of favouring a particular action, and this would be a big difference. The belief that one comes to in the light of reasoning would stand in a different relation to that reasoning from any relation that an action can stand, no matter how appropriate that action might be. But we should remember in all this that we are thinking not of the thing believed, but of the believing of it. It is the believing that is favoured, not the thing believed. A thing believed, whatever we take such a thing to be (and there is a long story to be told about that, which I am hoping largely to avoid) is not capable of being favoured by anything. It is the believing that we are thinking of here, which, unlike the thing believed, is a response. Now if we think that considerations can favour a particular believing in a way that they cannot favour a particular action, we are probably supposing that the believing is, as it were, particularized by its content—or perhaps better, by the thing believed. And the thing believed is indeed particular enough, I allow. But that is not enough to particularize the believing of it. For that believing is a response, and as such it will, just like an action, have various properties about which the considerations that favour it are silent. For instance, it can be done enthusiastically or reluctantly, it can be done sooner or later—and so on.

So the Prichard point applies to reasoning to belief as well as to reasoning to action; it creates no distinction between the two. One only supposes otherwise if one thinks in terms of the thing believed rather than of the believing of it. Once we remember that believing is as much a response as acting is, the Prichard point loses its bite. By this I do not mean that it is not significant, nor that we do not have to worry about it. I think it is significant, and that we do have to worry about it, because it is not at all clear to me that it makes sense to talk about favouring acting in a way. I don't know what sort of a thing this 'acting in a way' is, such that it can be favoured by anything. But that difficulty, which I take very seriously, is not one that this book needs to address. For whatever the answer to it, that answer will have to work equally well for what we might call 'believing in a way'.

2.4 Preliminary Conclusion

I have spent a certain amount of time on this point because it will be important later (in Chapter 8). But now I return to the main question, which is whether the relations between the considerations adduced in theoretical reasoning and the belief that is our response to those considerations are necessarily different from the relations between the considerations adduced in practical deliberation and the action that is our response to those considerations, or whether those relations might be the same. And the easy answer was that those relations may indeed be broadly the same. When an agent deliberates well and then acts accordingly, the action done is of the sort most favoured by the considerations rehearsed, taken as a whole—just as when an agent reasons well and then believes accordingly, the belief formed is of the sort most favoured by the considerations rehearsed. It is, as far as this goes, the same on both sides. So in whatever sense a belief can be of the sort called for by the reasoning, in that same sense an action can be of the sort called for by the reasoning—that is, by the considerations adduced, taken as a whole. And one can form a belief, or act, in the light of that fact.

Very many more such similarities will emerge as we go along. Favouring and disfavouring are not the only normative relations with which we will have to deal. I intend to show that the more complex the picture becomes, the stronger becomes my general answer to the Question: that action can stand in pretty much all the relations to the considerations adduced in reasoning in which belief can stand.

In this sense, then, one can reason to action just as much as one can reason to belief, and Aristotle's picture is secure. Should we express this point by saying that action can be the conclusion of practical reasoning and belief the conclusion of theoretical reasoning? The difficulties that emerged about the notion of a conclusion deter me from making this claim. A conclusion needs to be *drawn*. One cannot draw an action, but one cannot draw a belief either; that is not the worry here. More to the point is that there may be a difference between drawing the conclusion and believing in the way most favoured by the considerations adduced. In theoretical reasoning, there is always the possibility of seeing what follows from the considerations adduced, and in this sense drawing the relevant conclusion, but not yet accepting that conclusion. One can, after all, always decide to abandon one of the premises. Sometimes one sees what follows and for that reason rejects one of the considerations adduced—something must be wrong if this is where we are to end up. If so, we should perhaps distinguish between drawing the conclusion and concluding. Someone who concludes that p is someone who has gone beyond drawing the conclusion, in the sense above of seeing that it follows from what is on the table that p; to conclude that p is actually to accept that p. And presumably this same distinction can apply to practical reasoning. One can, for instance, see what course of action is called for by the considerations adduced, and for that reason look again in the hope that there has been some mistake or omission somewhere along the way.

So I would prefer not to say that Aristotle was right in thinking that action can be the conclusion of practical reasoning. But of course he did not have our notion of a conclusion; there is no really equivalent word in Greek. The word used in the passage I quoted in 1.3 actually means something like 'accomplished jointly'. So not much is lost by declining to express his position using the notion of a conclusion. Instead the passage might be retranslated as 'there are two beliefs, one universal and one about the particulars of the case; and when these are combined, the result of the combination (sc. that which is accomplished jointly) must in the one case be accepted/asserted, and in the practical case be done on the spot'.

I have already suggested that the notion of a conclusion is part of a small family of notions, which include the notions of a premise and of an inference. And I have already abandoned the idea that one can infer an action, and with that must go the idea that there can be premises for such an inference, and with that the idea that an action can be the conclusion of such an inference. But I would also say that one cannot infer a belief—understood as a believing—even if one can infer a 'thing to be believed'.

2.5 The Favouring Relation: Structure

I now turn to considering in more detail the nature of the favouring relation. To some extent this can be viewed as an independent enquiry into a matter of general interest. But my account of practical deliberation would be substantially incomplete without it. And if we get the favouring relation right, we are less likely to draw false contrasts between deliberation and (theoretical) reasoning.

The favouring relation is (at least) three-placed. There is *one place* for what is favoured—acting in a certain way, believing something or having some emotion. The list of things that can be favoured is as long as the list of possible responses. Only responses can be favoured. An emotion can be a response to a set of considerations adduced. Feeling that emotion, or having it, can be an appropriate response to the situation as one conceives it.

Now though (as I suggested in Chapter 1) an action perhaps cannot be broken up into two elements, the doing and the thing done, it can be broken up into two other elements, the agent and the doing. I understand an action as an agent causing a change, and the agent is one thing and the causing another. What is favoured is the causing of a change of a certain sort by a specific agent, or by any agent of a certain sort. So it is plausible that we should have a *second place* in the favouring relation, for an agent. A consideration might, for instance favour my acting in a certain way but not favour your acting in that way. That my wife is feeling upset is a reason for me to give her a hug and a kiss but it is not, I hope, a reason for anyone or everyone else to do so.

The *third place* is occupied by whatever does the favouring—what I have been calling 'the relevant consideration'. There can be no favouring without a favourer.

Tim Scanlon (2014: 30–1) thinks that there is also a place in the favouring relation for the relevant situation, since in different situations the same consideration may favour different responses. So his view is that the reasons-relation has four places, while I think it has only three. Here I am just going to assert that Scanlon's extra place is not necessary: the conditions for the obtaining of a relation will not all of them be part of that relation. So we can allow that what favours what may vary according to the nature of the situation at issue, without allowing that this means that the general situation occupies a place in that relation similar to that occupied by the agent, the consideration and the type of response favoured.

Now the relevant consideration is the thing that is doing the favouring, and we need to know what sort of thing can do that; with this we enter troubled waters. Here are two awkward points that I am going to defend in the next section. First, only something that is the case can favour anything. Second, no proposition can favour anything. There are of course such things as the proposition that *p*, and we must find a place and a role for them; but I will be suggesting that this role will not be the role of a favourer.

These are murky waters and before we plunge into them it is important to remember what has been achieved so far. We have found a way of sustaining Aristotle's position about the relation between theoretical and practical reasoning, which involved allotting a central role to the favouring relation. People do have different views about the favouring relation, but they pretty much all allow that some such relation exists, and that it has (at least) the three places I have listed. There is no real issue about the agent-place. The Prichard point, about which I am still uneasy, concerns the nature of what is favoured. It is the nature of the favourer, the thing that does the favouring, that remains to be investigated, and this is much more contested. What follows, then, is my account of the favourer.[4]

2.6 What Does the Favouring?

Propositions are capable of being true or being false, but no proposition can be the case, or be so. It is states of affairs that are the case, that obtain or are so. A state of affairs is not a true proposition, even though for each obtaining state of affairs there will be a true proposition to the effect that things are so. A true proposition is an accurate representation of some state of affairs. The world cannot, at least as ordinarily conceived,[5] consist entirely of propositions. There must be something in addition to the propositions, something for them to represent. These are states of affairs, real or otherwise. And in addition to the propositions and the states of affairs there are objects, and there are the ways those objects are, but their being that way is presumably a state of affairs again. The objects exist, but are not the case, nor are they capable of being true or false. Neither the objects, nor the ways they are, are propositions. (All these claims are controversial, but I have argued for them elsewhere (2000: ch. 5.2) and here I am merely laying my cards on the table.)

There are interesting asymmetries here, and propositions turn out to be the odd ones out. Objects exist, and when they do exist, their existence is normally[6] contingent; those that exist contingently can cease to exist, but when they do so there is not something still there that is failing to exist. If an object does not exist, there is no 'it' to have an alternative property of non-existence. So 'exists' is an odd sort of success term for objects. The analogous term for states of affairs is 'obtain', but here we hit the question whether there are some states of affairs that do not obtain. It may be that all states of affairs obtain (some contingently and others necessarily), so that if a state of affairs fails to obtain there is no 'it' to

---

[4] The views I will express here are largely the same as views I expressed in ch. 5 of my *Practical Reality*. I acknowledge, of course, that they are controversial. In the final chapter (10.6) I consider briefly what might happen to my overall view if I turn out to be mistaken on this point.

[5] Of course there are subtle philosophical views to the contrary, from Berkeley to Kit Fine and Ted Sider.

[6] I put the 'normally' here to allow for the possibility of non-contingent existents such as God is often supposed to be.

have the alternative property of non-obtainingness. Or it may be, as some suppose, that some states of affairs obtain and others don't. Luckily I do not officially have to pronounce on this question; it is enough for me that the considerations adduced in deliberation are states of affairs, real or supposed (which is to say: obtaining or merely supposed to obtain). And we should not forget that when people are acting in the light of certain considerations, the context is intensional. A consideration need not obtain, or be the case, for someone to act in its light. (The 'in-the-light-of' relation ushers in an intensional context; one can act in the light of a consideration that is not so.)

Finally, if events are distinct from states of affairs, they are things that can happen, and perhaps some happen contingently and others necessarily—and there may even be some events that don't happen. 'Happen' is the analogous success term for events.

Propositions have the special feature of being able to be either true or false; a false proposition is just as much a proposition as a true one. If propositions exist at all (which I take to be dubious since 'exist' is the success term for objects and it is not clear that propositions are objects), their existence is necessary rather than contingent. They do not have an analogous success term. Propositions are not capable of being the case, either, only of being true, which is quite different. So when we say 'it is the case that p', the 'that p' part of this cannot be in the business of specifying a proposition. It must specify a state of affairs, because only states of affairs can be the case.

With these complex preliminaries over, I maintain that only things that are the case can count in favour of (that is, be a reason for) a response. The simple reason for this is that it makes no sense to say 'that she is ill is a reason to call the doctor, but she is not ill'. The most we could mean is 'that she is ill would be a reason if she were, but she is not'. An object cannot count in favour of anything either, though the fact that it exists, or rather its existing (which is a state of affairs) can. So no objects are reasons. Can an event be a reason? I find it easier to think of the fact (or rather state of affairs) that the event happened as a reason than to think of the event itself as one. But I leave events aside here.

The real issue concerns propositions. A false proposition cannot be a reason on any account, but what about the true ones? Suppose that her illness, her being ill, is a reason to call the doctor. We might happily say this: that she is ill is a reason to call the doctor. This might merely be another way of saying that her being ill is a reason to call the doctor, and if so that reason would be a state of affairs. But might it mean instead, or in addition, that the true proposition that she is ill is a reason to call the doctor? We might be tempted to think that something that is true, namely that she is ill, is a reason to call the doctor—and the truth that she is ill, being distinct from her illness, will have to count as a true proposition. My view, however, is that the temptation to think in this way derives from the fact that we do not ordinarily distinguish with any consistency between 'something that is true' and 'something that is the case, or that is so'. So ordinary usage is little help to us here. What we are after is the metaphysics of the favouring relation. In trying to decide whether something that is true can be a reason for us to respond in one way or another, ordinary ways of speaking are not going to provide much of a solution.

If we are to make progress, then, perhaps the way to do so is to consider the sort of object that a proposition is supposed to be. Propositions represent the world as being a certain way. So propositions are representations of things as being thus and so. Now: can any representation itself be a reason? It is clear that the state of affairs represented can be a reason. But what about the representation itself? Some representations are themselves objects, which can be bought and sold and burnt and defaced; here I have in mind pictures, photographs, and the like. But these are objects, and no object is itself a reason. If a proposition is an object, it cannot be a reason either. But perhaps propositions are not to be counted as objects. A proposition is, as it were, naked representation— representation without any representing object. It is not that the proposition has certain (non-representational) properties in virtue of which it represents. That is how pictures and photographs manage to represent. They have non-representational properties in virtue of which they succeed in representing things as being this way rather than that. But propositions appear to have no intrinsic non-representational properties. Now how could such a thing count in favour of our responding to it in one way rather than another? Well, I admit that this is a rhetorical question, but it seems to me to have bite. I don't see how something that has only representational properties could count in favour of or against a response.

One could reply to this that only true propositions are favourers, but this seems to me to miss the point. If propositions are indeed capable of favouring, only the true ones can do it, I admit. But in such a case, it is not the proposition that favours, but its truth, or that it is true—and that a proposition is true is itself a state of affairs.

I conclude that propositions are not capable of standing on the left-hand side of the favouring relation. This role is played, and only played, by states of affairs.

2.7 Arguments from Error

But I have not yet considered in all this the main argument that the considerations adduced in deliberation *must* be propositions. The argument is that those considerations do not need to be the case for us to bring them to bear in deliberation, and only propositions are capable of surviving the relevant sort of failure. As I said above, there are no objects that fail to exist, there are no events that fail to happen and there are no states of affairs that fail to obtain. But propositions that fail to be true are still perfectly good propositions—just false ones. Falsehood is not a sort of ontological failure for propositions in the way that not happening is for events and not existing is for objects. So whether we are right or wrong about the matters from which we reason, that is, about the considerations we adduce, those considerations are certainly what we are reasoning from, and therefore they *must* be propositions, and cannot be restricted to states of affairs.

Put it another way: since our reasoning is good or bad in a way that has nothing to do with whether the considerations we reason from are the case/are true/obtain, those considerations must have the sort of status that is indifferent to such questions, and only propositions have that sort of status.

This style of argument has been extraordinarily influential, but in my view it is all a mistake. If people reason from considerations that are not the case, there is nothing whatever that counts in favour of their concluding as they do. But still their reasoning might be good, if it tracks the responses which the relevant considerations would have favoured, had they been the case. It is not that there is something that does count in favour of their conclusion, though unfortunately that something is not so. Rather, nothing counts in favour of their response, but in their reasoning they have tracked and correctly identified the way of acting that would have been most favoured if things had been as they supposed.

Of course one might retreat to saying that what they reason from is not what they believe (for it is what they believe that is failing to be the case here), but their believing it, or that they believe it. I will consider and reject this resort in the following section (3.1), where I will argue that the considerations on which we act are rarely that we believe this or that, and the considerations from which we reason are rarely that we believe this or that either.

Nonetheless if people reason from considerations that are not the case, it is not as if they are reasoning from nothing—from a kind of blank. It is for them as if those things were so, and they are reasoning in the light of that mistaken conception (that is, in the light of the way they mistakenly conceive things to be). So certainly it is not all a disaster. They have made one mistake, yes, but only one, and having made that mistake they then continue along pretty well, one might say. Their deliberation, given their starting point, may even be impeccable. But still it is all built on nothing.

It would be a different matter if what they reason from is the case, but they entirely mistake the practical relevance of those facts. That they are reasoning from things that are the case does not save their reasoning from being terrible. So we can have good reasoning that is built on nothing, and bad reasoning that is built on something solid.

Those who start from mistakes are still deliberating from the world as they take it to be—from supposed matters of fact or states of affairs. For them, it is as if things really are as they take them to be, and they deliberate on that basis. But the basis is still the things they take to be so, not their taking them to be so.

Finally: what if I am wrong in maintaining that propositions cannot favour anything? What difference would that make to what is to come? The difference it would make is that propositions could appear on the right-hand side of the grids. And then it would appear that the relations between them are all propositional, in a way that would encourage the view that the relations that hold reasoning together are all inferential (since inference is often conceived as tracking relations between propositions). And if they are inferential, it is very hard to see an ordinary action such as kicking a ball as the conclusion of anything worth calling an inference—which is the death of the Aristotelian programme. I don't say that it is impossible for that programme to survive, but it would be noticeably harder. I think we would have to say that propositions can bear non-inferential relations to each other, and to other things, which is just possible but hard to make stick.

I revisit this issue in the final chapter (10.5).

3

The Material Theory of Practical Reasoning

In the previous chapter I outlined what I call the 'formal theory' of practical reasoning. This amounted to placing the favouring relation at the centre of my account, and then giving an account of the structure of that relation. Practical reasoning takes us from the situation as we see it to acting in the way that is most favoured by that situation. And it does this *directly*. It does not need to pass through an intermediate stage, such as a belief that acting in this way is most favoured. The considerations adduced favour so acting, and we act in their light. This is exactly analogous to the functioning of theoretical reasoning, which takes us equally directly from considerations adduced to the adoption of that belief (that is, to believing in the way) which (we hope) is most favoured by the considerations adduced—which is to say, by the state of affairs (or the relevant aspects of the situation) as we see it. My Aristotelian view is that action is as direct, as unmediated a response to reasoning as belief can be.

In this chapter I lay out what I call the material theory of practical reasoning. This puts some flesh on the bare bones of structure. So far the things we reason from have been understood as a simple list of relevant considerations which together go to favour the response we adopt in their light. But it will turn out that there are much more interesting things to say than just that.

3.1 Mapping Reasoning

Now let us return to our grids:

Belief	p
Belief	q
So: Belief	r

This grid represents (rather minimally) an example of informal theoretical reasoning. One that would represent deliberation leading to action would look rather different:

Belief	p
Belief	q

So: Acts

The difference stems from our inability to break the action up into a doing and a thing done in a way that would suit the demands of the grid. Now what is favouring what here? It is not the believing that p and the believing that q that favours acting in the way we decide. It is what is believed, that p and that q. Though the believings can be understood as states of affairs, or perhaps events, and so are capable of serving as reasons, they are not likely to be our reasons in most cases. I asserted this in the final section of Chapter 2 but it needs a little argumentation.

When I believe that p, and act accordingly, the reason for which I act may be that p, or it may be that I believe that p. These are different reasons. The difference between them is easily shown by an example.[1] Suppose I believe that everyone is out to get me. There are two very different ways in which I might respond. I might go into hiding in the hope that people will gradually lose interest. Or I might make an appointment to see a psychiatrist. If I do the former, my reason will be that (as I believe) everyone is out to get me. If I do the latter, my reason will not be that they are all out to get me; if that were my reason, I should be as suspicious of the psychiatrist as of everyone else. My reason will be that I believe they are all out to get me, and I can do something about that.

The same point can be made about desiring. Suppose that I desire to V, and act accordingly. The reason for which I act may be that I desire to V, or it may be something to do with V-ing. A familiar example: I desire to kill my parents, and so I go out to buy some poison to put in their tea. Alternatively, again, I might make an appointment with a psychiatrist, or take a course of cold baths. In the latter case, my reason for what I do is genuinely that I want to kill my parents, or my wanting to do so; it is not the thing I want but that I want it. In the former case, it is something else.

[1] I apologize here to those familiar with my earlier work, especially chs 5–6 of my *Practical Reality* (2000).

We see then that ordinarily we reason, not from our believing this or that, but from what we believe, that p or that q. And the reasons for which we then act are, not surprisingly, the same as the considerations that we bring to bear in deliberation and which we eventually take to favour most the course of action on which we decide. So the considerations that favour acting in this way rather than that appear on the right-hand side of the grid. That we believe those things to be the case has its own relevance, but is not itself among the considerations normatively relevant to our choice of action.

So as far as the practical grid goes, we will want to map the favouring relation like this:

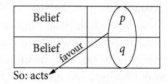

One complication to note here is that the grid falls far short of displaying every aspect of our deliberation. (The feature that follows can be added to those mentioned at the end of the Introduction to this chapter and in 1.10.) For instance, the grid does not display the attention we give to rejected alternatives. Ordinarily we consider several alternative actions, or at least several alternative ways of achieving the same result, and none of that is displayed here. So what one might call the comparative aspect of deliberation is hidden. What we have is rather the eventual result: the action we decide on and the considerations that counted in favour, or that we took to count in favour. So the comparative aspect of deliberation, which should certainly not be forgotten, is left out of account in our grid. I don't think this is worrying, exactly, but it is worth remembering.

Putting those complications aside, the position we have now reached is this. In practical reasoning we assemble considerations relevant to our choice of action and, if things go well, we act in the way most favoured by those considerations taken together. This is exactly the same as what happens in theoretical reasoning, where, again, we assemble considerations relevant to what to believe and, if things go well, do end up adopting the view most favoured by those considerations. Remember that what is favoured is not the view adopted but adopting that view, since what is favoured is always a response of some sort. This similarity between practical and theoretical reasoning is at the heart of my account of the practical. It is practical because the relevant response is an action, and it is reasoning because of the ways in which the relevant considerations relate to each other in making the case for this, rather than that, response.

So far, however, I have been thinking entirely in terms of the favouring relation, and this may have given the impression that this is the whole of the story. That is far from being the case, because in addition to the favouring relation there are other ways in which considerations can affect the case for acting. I now turn to elaborate this point.

3.2 Different Forms of Relevance

One aspect worthy of comment is that as we have mapped it, it is the considerations taken together that are shown as favouring the course of action that we decide on. This is not meant to rely on the fact, which I announced at the outset, that deliberation is a more complex matter than simply acting for a reason. Deliberation is also a more complex matter than 'simply' acting for several reasons at once. There are two sides to this. The first is the comparative side. I may have several reasons for doing one thing and several reasons for doing another, and I have to work out the combined strength of each team, as it were, in order to see which is the stronger. But there is a second source of complication, hidden behind the word 'combined'. This is the fact—as I take it to be—that a case for doing something does not just consist of reasons to act in that way. The case must include some reasons of that sort, I would suppose. But it may also contain considerations which, though they make a considerable difference to the strength of the case overall, do not contribute to it as independent reasons. Their role is different from that of a reason.

In previous sections I have concentrated on the favouring relation. I have tried to show that it is as central to theoretical reasoning as to practical deliberation, and I have expressed (with what will no doubt appear to some to be inadequate argument) views about the structure and the metaphysics of the favouring relation. But now I am broadening the general account of reasoning that I am offering. Reasoning is not just a matter of producing reasons and trying to work out which side is stronger. It is much more interesting than that. The favouring relation brings with it all sorts of supporting relations, and if we want to understand how a case is built, we need to be aware of those other relations and the different differences they can make.

There are various ways in which this point can be made. We might say that though the building of a case for action (or for belief) is fairly simple in structure, still there remain other relations involved in the assessment and defence of that case. We might say that not all reasons function in the same sort of way. Or we might say that in the making of a case, we need to consider a range of different normative relations that cluster round, but are not reducible to, the notion of a reason, or favourer. I associate these three possibilities with Stephen Toulmin, Joseph Raz, and my own earlier work. In what follows I merely lay out that work in order to show its relevance to our general conception of reasoning. The general idea is that, even when we have come to agreement on the nature of the favouring relation, there remains much to be done if we are to understand the ways in which considerations that are not all relevant in the same sort of way may still combine to make a case for or against action. And it will be important that exactly the same can be said about making a case for or against belief.

We can distinguish between what I am calling the formal theory of reasoning and the material theory of reasoning. So far, in this and the previous chapter, I have been discussing the formal theory. I have asked what sorts of things are capable of being reasons, and about the structure of the favouring relation. But the favouring relation is not the only relation in play in reasoning, just as it is not the only relation relevant to our account of how it is that a case for action is built. As we will see, a case for action can be strengthened by the addition of something that is not an independent reason for doing the action. So good reasoning requires a sensitivity to reasons, but it requires much more than that. The material theory is interested in laying out all the different ways in which a consideration can make a difference to the strength of a case.

3.3 Beyond Favouring (1): Toulmin

Toulmin's third book, *The Uses of Argument*, starts with a distinction between substantive and formal argumentation. (This distinction between substantive and formal is not the same as the distinction I have just drawn between material and formal.) Formal argumentation is the sort of thing we read about in logic textbooks; formal approaches cast all relevant considerations as premises, and view all reasoning as aiming at the perfection of formal validity. Substantive argumentation is what we find in practice in the law courts—and, I would say, in ordinary practical reasoning. Toulmin insisted that substantive reasoning in general aims to show only that it would be *reasonable* to believe its conclusion, rather than that rationality *requires* those who accept the premises to accept the conclusion. But this notion of the reasonable, which comes in degrees, need not be taken as distinct from that of what conclusion we have good, or most, reason to accept. Toulmin was fairly obsessed with the inability of formal logic to serve as a general account of reasoning, and I have a lot of sympathy with him on this point.

Formal logic is peculiar in many respects. One aspect is that all premises in a properly formulated argument without redundancy are equally important. Take any one away and the argument becomes straightforwardly invalid—as useless as such an argument can be. It is interesting in this respect to think of the 'share of the total' account of contribution. Suppose we are trying to assess the contribution of each person working in a factory. We might try to work out how much of the total output can be attributed to each worker (perhaps so as to decide who is to be paid more). But this approach doesn't work if each worker is essential, because the subtraction method of seeing how much less would be produced without that worker gives the same answer for each: the entire product is attributable to each worker, because without that worker there would be no product at all. The same picture applies to each of the premises in a formally valid argument.

Second, and consequently, one might suppose that all premises in a formally valid argument do the same sort of job. Each of them turns something of no value at all into something rationally compelling.

Toulmin thought that substantive argumentation is completely different in both of these respects. Different 'premises' do different sorts of thing, and a good argument can be made even better by the addition of appropriate considerations.

For present purposes the main contribution of Toulmin's book lay in the distinctions it drew between several different ways in which considerations can be relevant to a conclusion (rather than the logician's catchall 'premises'): as data, warrant, backing, rebuttal, or qualifier. These distinctions offered ways of mapping and understanding the different sorts of substantial argumentation to be found in ethics, in the law, and in science. They thereby offered new tools to the students of rhetoric, who eagerly embraced them, to the extent that they became a dominant paradigm in that field.

What follows is my own example of these distinctions at work. John Smith has died and left his chess set to his brother Bill. The datum is that John Smith's will says 'I leave my chess set to my brother Bill Smith', and the conclusion is that Bill should have the chess set. The warrant for that conclusion is that people should receive what they are left in a valid will. The backing for that warrant is the current state of inheritance law in the relevant jurisdiction. A qualifier is something that assesses the strength of the argument. Such a qualifier might be 'at least prima facie'.[2] So our case might establish our conclusion only prima facie; we make a 'prima facie' case at best. A rebuttal of that case would consist in a later valid will. So we could understand the qualifier as 'unless there is a later will'— which of course there often is.

With these distinctions in hand, Toulmin wanted to say that reasoning of this sort is not rationally compelling in the way that a formally valid deductive argument is supposed to be compelling, but still the case made can be one that is more or less reasonable—or, we might just say, stronger or weaker. Rational compellingness (or compulsion) is all or nothing, but reasonableness is a matter of degree. Substantive argumentation will never achieve any sort of compellingness; we cannot say of a good case that it is fairly compelling, meaning by this that it has a little bit of compellingness, but not as much as a valid deductive argument would have; and we cannot say even of a very good case that it is as reasonable as a case can be. There may be no such thing as perfection available.

I don't see much to complain about in these distinctions of Toulmin's, nor in his distinction between reasonableness and rational compellingness. One of the attractions of Toulmin's work here is that one could map an argument in the law on the page, as it were, using his distinctions. One could imagine circling a sentence and writing 'warrant' in the margin, and circling another and writing 'qualifier' against that one. In that way one could see Toulmin's distinctions at work, and in that way come to understand in greater detail how reasonableness is built, how the force of

---

[2] This is not 'prima facie' in the famous sense given to that phrase by W. D. Ross (1930, ch. 2.).

an argument is made. This seems to me to be a highly desirable outcome, and one that could inspire further efforts in the same direction.

For even if one allows the relevance, and the importance, of Toulmin's distinctions, he left the notion of the data uninvestigated. There are indeed the things that stand as data for the conclusion in argumentation, but the notion of the data is really a black box into which Toulmin does not look. He does however say (1956: 102) that two facts can both be relevant to the conclusion, but relevant in different ways, and this is a hint on which we can build. Work by Raz and myself has looked at the ways in which reasons work, and found further distinctions which themselves could be marked on the page in the way that Toulmin's can.

3.4 Beyond Favouring (2): Raz and Exclusionary Reasons

Joseph Raz's main contribution in this connection is the notion of an exclusionary reason, which first appeared in his (1975a and 1975b). This notion is offered in pursuit of the idea that not all reasons do the same job. So even if all data (in Toulmin's sense) are reasons, not all reasons are equal, and it may be profitable to investigate such distinctions between them as present themselves. There is a picture of reasons as counting in favour of some conclusion, which has it that this is all that a reason can do. But Raz's exclusionary reasons do something to other reasons: they exclude those others from consideration, preventing them somehow from having the sort of practical relevance they might be expected to have, even though they remain as reasons. An exclusionary reason is a reason not to act on some other reason, which it has 'excluded'. So if there are exclusionary reasons, it is not always true that one ought to do what one has most reason to do. It is not always a matter of more or less.

The classic example of an exclusionary reason is an order from a competent authority, say a superior officer in the armed forces. A soldier might have very good reasons not to obey this order, but somehow those reasons are not to be acted on, in the light of the order. Orders do not outweigh other considerations; they are not especially weighty reasons. A soldier is not expected to think 'Well I have lots of good reasons not to do this, but there is this one very strong reason to do it.' The order does not leave him with this sort of choice.

This is not quite the way that Raz presented his distinction originally. There he started by distinguishing first-order and second-order reasons. A second-order reason is a reason that concerns how we are to treat or respond to a first-order reason. It is not as such a first-order reason. But the superior officer's order was a first-order reason. How are we to sort this out? One answer is that this first-order reason is also a second-order reason. The order is both a reason to do what one is ordered to do and a reason not to take into account other first-order reasons. An ordinary first-order reason to V is not itself a reason not to do actions inconsistent with V-ing, nor is it a reason not to consider opposing reasons. As we might put it, a consideration that speaks in favour of V-ing does not thereby speak against all other courses of action, nor does it speak for or against how one is to respond to other reasons. But exclusionary reasons are different.

One of Raz's first examples of an exclusionary reason was a promise only to take into account certain reasons. Unlike the command, this promise is only a second-order reason—a reason to treat other reasons in a certain way.

Now some people are not convinced that the phenomena Raz is pointing to are really distinctive enough to call for this very radical treatment. For present purposes, I don't really need to adjudicate on this issue. More to my point would be the question where on Toulmin's map we should locate these exclusionary reasons if there are any. It does not seem to me that they belong squarely in the data box. The data, one would have thought, are first-order reasons that it is right to treat as such; and exclusionary reasons (if there are any) determine which considerations are of that sort. They are not themselves further data. So perhaps they should be placed somewhere else. But where? The question is especially pressing because Toulmin's own example is taken from the law, where the notion of a reason why other reasons are not to be admitted finds an especially welcoming environment. But it need not detain us here.

3.5 Beyond Favouring (3): Enabling/Disabling and Intensifying/Attenuating

Distinctions which I myself have stressed in previous work (stemming back to 1983, but conveniently summarized in my 2004a: ch. 2) are more squarely located in the data box than anywhere else, but are still not distinctions between different types of data, if we understand a datum as an independent reason. Starting from the suggestion that a consideration that is a reason in one case need not be a reason in another (which is not the same as saying that it need not be as strong a reason, something which I think all would be willing to allow), I argued that in such a case there would need to be an explanation of how this had come about, and such an explanation would be likely to appeal to a feature of the second case which prevented the relevant consideration from being there the reason that it had been in the first, or a feature of the first case that enabled that consideration to be there the reason that it is not elsewhere. The terms I produced for such features were 'enablers' and 'disablers'; they enable other features to be reasons or disable something that is a reason elsewhere, or even normally, from being so here. Enablers and disablers need not themselves be reasons—just as Raz's second-order reasons did not need to be first-order reasons; remember the promise example. But again like Raz's second-order reasons, a disabler or an enabler could itself be a reason. If it were a reason, it would then be playing two roles. It would favour some conclusion, and it would enable some other consideration to do the same or disable it from doing so.

This distinction between enabling and disabling is an all-or-nothing matter, really, since either something is a reason or it is not. One might say that the distinction between enabling and disabling is like the distinction between switching on and switching off, which is not a matter of degree. Something cannot be to some extent a reason but to some extent not, nor to some extent on and to some extent off. But there is also a distinction to be considered here which is a matter of degree. Sometimes one consideration can intensify, or strengthen, the reason given us by another; and others may weaken or attenuate that reason without destroying it altogether. So there can be intensifiers and there can be attenuators. Considerations that intensify or attenuate the reasons given us by others do not themselves need to be reasons in order to play those roles. But they might be; a consideration might both count in favour of a course of action and alter the strength of other reasons relevant to the case.

What is more, an enabler can itself be disabled, that is, prevented from doing its enabling job. And a disabler can be disabled too. Equally, a consideration can be turned into a disabler, or an enabler, by the presence of some further consideration. Whether these things happen often or not, they seem to be possible. And the same applies to attenuators and intensifiers. If it is only in certain circumstances that a certain consideration intensifies the favouring done by another, that means that some aspect of those circumstances is acting as an enabler for that intensification.

Again, then, the question is where on Toulmin's map these distinctions should appear. They fit exactly his remark that though all these considerations are relevant, they are not relevant in the same way. The crucial point is that something does not need to be itself a reason in order to affect the fate of other supposed reasons by enabling, disabling, attenuating, or intensifying them. It seems to me therefore that the simplest answer is that Toulmin's list of categories is incomplete—which we could probably have predicted anyway.[3]

3.6 Pulling These Strands Together

After this long discussion of Toulmin, Raz, and my own work, we can now return to the main theme. I was discussing the significance of the phrase 'the relevant considerations taken together', and the nature of the things suited to appear on the right-hand side in our grid. We now see that such considerations can be many and various, and their forms of relevance may also vary greatly. Many of them could not normally be considered premises, if by that we mean considerations that all play the same kind of role. If we were, for instance, to restrict entries on the right-hand side to those that stand as reasons for or against our conclusion, we would certainly be excluding many considerations that play a vital role in determining the strength of the case for this or that response. So the appearance given by the last grid shown—

Belief	p
Belief	q

So: acts

---

[3] I should confess here, to my shame, that I have only recently lit upon (thanks to Ralf Bader) an incredible early paper by Robert Nozick which is replete with further similar distinctions; see Nozick (1968, esp. §VII).

—that on the right-hand side there are nice free-standing nuggets, each making a separate contribution but all making contributions of the same sort, is quite wrong. In the right-hand column we are to put anything whatever that might be relevant to what to do. This might even include things that the deliberator decides eventually to discount. After all, deliberation is a process, and part of that process is the attempt to work out what is relevant to what, and in what way. So the apparently static state represented by the grid can at best be a snapshot of a frozen segment of the deliberative process. If it is a frozen segment of a process, it might contain not only the considerations that themselves favour the action to be done, but also those discounted considerations that favoured some other course of action. The agent, in recounting her deliberation, might say, 'I did it for these reasons and despite these other considerations, which I decided were not important enough to make a difference.' If so, the considerations in the right-hand column will need to include some that favoured an alternative course of action. The nature and relevance of despite-clauses are often ignored, but should not be.

Alternatively we can take the grid to represent the end-state of that process, or perhaps better a sort of idealization of that end-state, in which the mutual relevances of the various contributors have all been sorted out and tempting irrelevances omitted. At that point, the deliberator has determined the case for V-ing and is set to V in the light of that. At this stage one might reasonably omit all reference to all those things despite which one came to act as one did, and the grid then delineates simply the case for the action decided upon, or to be decided upon. We might think that this sort of idealization is what is involved when we ask what course of action is 'most favoured by the considerations adduced, taken together'. But that question can now be seen to be misleading. The 'considerations adduced' need not all individually favour that course of action, even if they are part of a complex picture of the situation under which that course of action, that practical response, is more favoured than is any other. So we should avoid asking what course of action is most favoured by the considerations adduced, taken together. The relevant favouring will almost always be done by only some of those considerations, while the others play some supporting role—or, if they are despite-clauses, not even that. What emerges as most favoured in the light of all the considerations adduced should not be thought of as what is most favoured by all those considerations, taken together. I issue this warning note in the hope that I myself have nowhere fallen into this trap, which is easily done.

As we will see when we come to consider instrumental reasoning, sometimes things are much simpler than they may be elsewhere. But instrumental reasoning has no special status in this connection; it certainly does not constitute the whole of practical reasoning, as I understand the matter, despite what so many people have said.

In Chapter 4 I show how the various forms of theoretical reasoning— in particular, formal and probabilistic—can perfectly well be understood in the way in which we are now understanding practical reasoning. There will be differences between practical and theoretical reasoning, but those differences are to be found in the ways in which we explain the various normative relations that play the driving role in the making of a case for doing, or believing, this rather than that. The structures are the same, but the explanations are not. But this is just a promissory note.

3.7 Mapping Reasoning (the Material Theory)

As I have presented things, in practical reasoning we start from considerations whose practical relevance can be of various sorts, and end up acting in the way that we take, in the light of those considerations, to be more favoured than is any alternative way of acting.[4]

On this showing, practical reasoning is not any form of logic. Logic does not recognize the difference between the different forms of relevance (enabling, disabling, etc.), and it is not interested in the favouring relation.

But that doesn't matter. We were not trying to turn practical reasoning into the application of a practical logic. We were trying to take practical reasoning on its own terms, and to try to understand how that process can build up a picture of the situation facing us that has a certain practical significance, or force. It is in response to, and in recognition of, the situation as so shaped that we take this course of action rather

---

[4] I will consider later (8.5) the question how to characterize reasoning that throws up two equally good alternatives and the choice that results. For the moment I am focusing, perhaps optimistically, on cases in which the reasoning does indeed deliver one most favoured alternative.

than any alternative. The sort of significance involved is not logical force—if there is any such thing, which I doubt. If there is any force involved, it is the force of the favouring relation. What leads us to take this course of action in preference to others available is that this course of action is more favoured by the situation, taken as a whole, than is any alternative.[5]

This may make it appear that we need first to believe that this course of action is the one most favoured by the considerations we adduce, and only then to act in that light, which would have the effect of inserting a theoretical conclusion between our practical reasons and the action that is our response to them. That this understanding is not the only possible one is shown by the fact that one could make the same move with respect to acting for a simple reason, holding that in order to act in the light of a consideration as a reason, we must first believe it to be a reason. My own view is that any such suggestion over-intellectualizes the case, since one does not need to have the concept of a reason in order to respond to a consideration as a reason. For the same reason, we should not suppose that to act in the light of a group of considerations, taken as a whole, one needs to believe that together they make the best case. The 'in the light of' relation should not be supposed to interpose a theoretical stage—a reasons-belief or a most-reasons-belief—into the passage from considerations to practical response. This point, which is of course vital to any assessment of the differences between my neo-Aristotelian approach and other more standard accounts, will reappear later, in Chapter 8.

So if we want an account of the force of practical reasoning, the notion of the favouring relation gives us what we are looking for. It comes in degrees, and our response to the situations that confront us is a response to those aspects of the situation that together favour one form of response more than any other form of response is favoured, either by the same or by other considerations.

Many people would want something called reasoning to have a discernible structure. All the other sorts of reasoning that we know—formal reasoning, for instance, or probabilistic reasoning, of which we will hear

---

[5] This is slightly incautious, because if there are enticing reasons one may be quite properly enticed actually to do something when another option is more enticing; there is no rational demand that one do the most enticing thing. On the possibility of such enticing reasons, see my (2004b).

a lot more shortly, clearly have some sort of structure which it is possible to expose, and the exposition of which serves to show how the reasoning works to support its conclusion. We can, as it were, reveal the machinery at work.

Practical reasoning, on my showing, seems to have little of that sort of structure. But that does not mean that it has no structure at all. It does have a structure, and in revealing that structure we can, as it were, reveal the machinery of that reasoning at work. Or at least we know something of its structure, and we can hope to find out more. The study of this sort of informal—that is, non-formal—reasoning is in its comparative infancy. But some advances have been made, as I tried to show in 3.3–3.6. We can use the distinctions that I outlined there in order to map the interrelations between the various elements of our reasoning, and these interrelations constitute a perfectly acceptable form of structure—or shape. The ideal, of course, is eventually to have a (more or less) complete knowledge of the different ways in which considerations can relate to each other in the construction of a good case for action. Progress in that direction would be progress in the material theory of reasoning, using the distinction between formal and material from 3.2 above; but the purpose of constructing the material theory is to use the distinctions it collects for the analysis of actual instances of reasoning. As is, I hope, becoming clear, I would like to be able to take any passage of practical reasoning, and to be able to map the way it works in the margin, noting the various instances of each possible relation as they occur.[6] This is the purpose of the material theory, which uses the distinctions it develops to map the way in which particular cases of reasoning work. We are a long way from that yet, but I see no reason to suppose that the attempt is either pointless or impossible. And the attempt is worthwhile because it is the attempt to build up a complete material theory of reasoning.

In recent years, therefore, I have been trying to find long passages of practical reasoning on which to practise my mapping skills. Part of my hope has been that in finding relations that would not fit into any of the boxes I had already identified, I would gradually be forced to expand my repertoire and thus, bit by bit, inch closer to a complete tool-chest (i.e. a complete material theory). The main difficulty, however, has been

---

[6] An early effort of this sort is to be found in the later chapters of Toulmin et al. (1979).

to locate a sufficient supply of suitably complex cases. I originally thought that the obvious place to look was to the law, and in particular to judgments of the Appeal Court, taking it that the most complex cases are likely to be those that get that far up the judicial ladder. Joseph Raz kindly guided me to some cases, and to some Law Lords, whom he thought probably to be worth this sort of attention. I am sad to report, however, that nothing of interest has yet emerged. The written judgments were often impressively long, which looked promising, but large parts of the judgments usually consisted of an elaborate laying out of the case at issue, and then a statement of the judgment itself. The reasoning was usually fairly brief—one paragraph or two at the most. I remember one that was of the form 'We just don't do things this sort of way in Britain.' So I have been forced to look elsewhere, and more recently I have turned to the great novelists, in particular to Anthony Trollope, who is especially good at revealing the twists and turns of people caught in an intractable dilemma.[7]

And I have found some promising material there, though I confess that my enquiries remain at best ongoing. To whet your appetite, here is an example from Trollope's *The Eustace Diamonds* (ch. 27):

One of the elder Fawn girls had assured her that under no circumstances could a lady be justified in telling a gentleman that he had spoken an untruth, and she was not quite sure that the law so laid down was right. And then she could not but remember that the gentleman in question was Lord Fawn, and that she was Lady Fawn's governess. But Mr. Greystock was her affianced lover, and her first duty was to him. And then, granting that she herself had been wrong in accusing Lord Fawn of untruth, she could not refrain from asking herself whether he had not been much more wrong in saying in her hearing that Mr. Greystock was not a gentleman. And his offence had preceded her offence, and had caused it! She hardly knew whether she did or did not owe an apology to Lord Fawn, but she was quite sure that Lord Fawn owed an apology to her.

The fact is that in the present deplorable state of the theory of reasoning we are entirely unable to reveal the rational coherence of this train of thought.

---

[7] Another interesting suggestion, which I owe to George Mason, is to look at diarists, perhaps political diarists such as Peter Mandelson or Alistair Campbell. When I have finished this book, that is what I will be doing.

3.8 Building a Practical Shape

So let us recognize that the beliefs (that is to say, the things we believe) from which we reason, from which we start in deliberation, may have any of various forms of relevance to our practical question what to do. We want to work out how to respond to the situation that confronts us, and to do that we have to build up a practical shape for the situation; that is to say, we have to come to understand so far as possible the ways in which the various relevant aspects of that situation relate to each other in the construction of an overall picture of what matters here that will enable us to determine how to respond. Until we understand, or are at least sensitive to, the relevant aspects of the situation and the ways in which they interact, we have little hope of lighting on the most appropriate response. And once we do have that understanding—even though it be only implicit—our deliberative work is pretty much done. Luckily an implicit understanding may be available to others than the theorist, or else most of us would be adrift without a paddle, for an implicit understanding is all that most can reasonably hope for. A sense that one consideration matters more than another is not something that needs articulation if it is to make the relevant difference to our decision. And an overall picture of the practical situation is rarely going to be articulate. In most cases, all we can really claim is that, if things go well, then as we consider the various aspects of our difficulty, one way of responding to them begins to present itself as the most appropriate, and our deliberation ends in that response.

One interesting apparent difference between deliberation, as I conceive it, and formal reasoning at the other end of the spectrum is that in formal reasoning the only real question is whether the premises taken together make the conclusion inevitable; there is no such thing as a force of argument that grows as one proceeds. There is absolutely no pressure on one to accept the conclusion until the final moment, when everything is in place. Take one premise out and the whole thing falls to the ground in ruins. But in practical reasoning the various relevant considerations can interact with each other in interestingly cumulative ways so as to make one decision more appropriate than another, and this means that there is something that grows as we go along. The main instances of something that can grow are the strength of the overall case for action, or the strength of certain reasons already on the table—or, of course, of certain difficulties.

These considerations combine to offset any sense that if there is no logical structure to practical deliberation, there is no structure at all. Of course there are pictures of reasoning under which there is little structure, even if there is a sense in which the case for a certain response can grow. A kitchen scales conception of reasoning, whether practical or theoretical, under which each consideration arrives with a weight which it deposits in the 'for' or the 'against' pan, would allow the growth of a case for action, or for belief, even if that growth had no very interesting structure since no consideration could affect the weight of any other. It would all be a simple matter of more or less. But few really take such a model seriously.

Still, the more one stresses the different ways in which considerations can be relevant to one's decision, the harder it may become to get the interrelations right. We may fear that the most we will be able to do is to list them, rather than to put them into any sort of shape or order. But some forms of relevance actually require a certain ordering, that is, putting these before those. If there is intensifying, it seems sensible to put the consideration intensified first, so as to display the sense in which what comes next (the intensifier) alters something that was already on the table (the reason intensified). And there are other ways in which it can matter how we approach a practical problem. Putting things in a wrong order may make it the harder to see the solution that together they call for (that is, the one that when properly put together they can be seen to support).

3.9 The Importance of the Order

So consider this scenario. You are the Chair of your Department. One day you learn, to your dismay, that one of your senior colleagues has apparently plagiarized the work of one of his own graduate students. Immediately you can see a whole host of practical problems arising, and your heart sinks. Your immediate question is how to respond to what you have been told. What you know so far is just this:

1 Your colleague plagiarized his graduate's work.

(I don't mean that this is all you know. Of course you may know all sorts of things that may or may not be relevant, such as the personalities involved, the past history of such events, if any, and so on. But this is what, starting from that sort of background knowledge, now arrives as new information to be dealt with.)

Then you learn

2   The student explicitly allowed him to do it.

This of course makes a difference—but what that difference is remains to be determined. Then you learn

3   The student didn't want him to do it.

So now consider the relation between the three things you have learnt so far. It is as if the first thing is what sets you your practical problem, and the second thing affects matters by altering the nature of the problem set you by the first. It also alters the nature of an appropriate response to the first. Some answers to the problem set by your colleague's action become less favoured, or cease to be favoured at all. The third thing does more of the same, that is, it alters the alteration made by the second. And similar changes are effected by this:

4   He didn't want to do it either.

By now one might be forgiven a certain degree of bewilderment as to what on earth has been going on. But there is at least a sort of shape involved here. The first thing you learnt sets you a problem, and the later things, as they come in, alter the sort of response that might be appropriate given what is on the table already. And they do this in a way quite different from the sort of alteration made by the introduction of a new reason.

Things are different if one starts from:

1   My mother has become seriously ill

Here my question is: should I drop everything and hurry to her bedside? Then I learn:

2   My father has fallen and broken his hip.

This looks like a new reason for me to rush off to the parental home, but it also makes a difference to the first reason, since he is now unable to care for her. So the second thing is functioning both as an independent reason and as an intensifier for the first reason. Because it is an independent reason, one might perfectly well have put it first. So here the order is less important.

The overall message here is that deliberation is given a shape by the operation of the various distinctions I introduced earlier in this chapter. And that shape is not just a shape in deliberation; our deliberation reveals (we hope) a shape that really belongs to the situation that confronts us. Deliberation is the process by which the practical shape of our predicament is uncovered, and in the process of deliberation we acquire our sense of how to respond to it, a sense that we express in action. It is this way of looking at things that is expressed in the title of this book.

4

From the Practical to the Theoretical

In this chapter I show how the various forms of theoretical reasoning—in particular, formal and probabilistic—can perfectly well be understood in the sort of way in which we are now understanding practical reasoning. There will be differences between practical and theoretical reasoning, but those differences are to be found in the ways in which we explain the various normative relations that play the driving role in the making of a case for doing, or believing, this or that. The structures are the same, but the explanations are not.

4.1 Formally Valid Deductive Reasoning

I suspect that in many readers the thought will have been growing that, on this showing, practical reasoning is nothing like theoretical reasoning at all. But I want to say that in all essentials, practical and theoretical reasoning are the same. What goes wrong is that people tend to have an over-narrow conception of theoretical reasoning, one that practical reasoning does not fit at all, and they therefore announce that there is no practical analogue of theoretical reasoning, and so no such thing as practical reasoning.

Not everyone responds in this way, of course, to the suggestions I have been making. Some say that there is practical reasoning, but it is reasoning from intention to intention. Others say that if there is such a thing as practical reasoning, it is reasoning to a 'practical belief', that is, a belief that one ought to act in such and such a way, or that one has most, or enough, reason so to act. These suggestions will be considered in due course (in Chapters 8 and 9). But I am trying to make the case that there can be reasoning to action as much as to belief or to intention.

My main argument is that action can stand in just the same central relations to the considerations adduced as can belief, or the formation of intention. Just like actions, both beliefs and intentions can be responses of the sort most favoured by the considerations that do favour them, in a way that reasoning can reveal, and they can be formed or adopted in that light.

Obviously, to take this line, I have to tell a more detailed story about theoretical reasoning, and about reasoning to an intention, than I have told as yet. And in telling that story, I will be taking it as significant that the distinctions between favouring and disfavouring, between enabling and disabling, and between intensifying and attenuating, apply just as much to reasoning to belief and to reasoning to intention as they do to reasoning to action. But these distinctions have no relevance to formally valid deductive reasoning. So let us first consider what sort of story to tell about that.

Deductive reasoning or inference, when it is not toy inference but has some serious purpose, is normally inference from things believed to things to be believed. So let us take a simple case of *modus ponens* to work with:

Belief	p
Belief	If p then q
Belief	q

If this is reasoning from beliefs to belief, and it is sound (as in this case of course it is), the conclusion-belief must be favoured by the considerations adduced. And so it is. We might even say that it is, as it were, conclusively favoured. The considerations adduced are that p and that if it is true that p then it is true that q. The considerations taken together favour believing that q, So far, so good. Now what are the things that are doing the favouring? It is natural to say that they are propositions. This is propositional logic, after all, so what we find on the right-hand side should be propositions. But I have already argued that propositions cannot favour anything. If they cannot do this in daily life, they cannot do it in logic either. So the things on the right-hand side of the grid above cannot be (being treated as) propositions; they must be (being treated as) states of affairs. And there is nothing wrong with that; that if it is true that p, it is also true that q, is as good a state of affairs as any.[1]

With this in hand we can add to our grid by inserting a representation of the favouring relation: the things that are doing the favouring and the thing that is favoured by them. So what is favoured is believing that q, and what favours believing that q is that p and that if it is true that p, it is also true that q. The grid now looks like this:

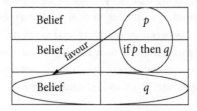

The story so far says nothing about propositions. But this is propositional logic, and surely there is some fact about propositions that plays a significant role in the story. Indeed there is. For when we are told that what favours believing that q is that p and that if it is true that p, it is also true that q, where these favourers are taken to be states of affairs rather than propositions, we are still going to want some explanation of the ability of these two considerations to favour believing that q, And this is where propositions might come in, for the explanation of that favouring might itself appeal to a relation between propositions. There are, after all, three propositions at play in our simple example, and the relation between those propositions (which are in fact merely a matter of form in this case, since we might as well have put '1', 'if 1 then 2', and '2') is what explains why the first two things believed favour believing the third. What explains the ability of the considerations adduced to favour believing the conclusion that q is the structural relation between the three propositions involved. This can be added to our grid, thus:

---

[1] There is an interesting question how to conceive of this reasoning if we take the conditional 'if p then q' as a rule licensing transition from believing that p to believing that q, rather than as a state of affairs.

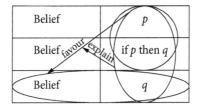

Note that the way in which I have represented the favouring relation on the grid above requires me effectively to erase the line between the two sides of the bottom line. It is not just the left-hand side, the believing, that is favoured, nor just the right-hand side, *q*, that is favoured. What is favoured is believing that *q*. So we see that, properly understood, the grid for theoretical reasoning is more like the grid for practical reasoning than we have been allowing.

Propositional logic, on this showing, is concerned with reasoning whose force is *explained* in a certain way, by relations between propositions; but this does nothing to show that one is reasoning from proposition to proposition. In reasoning, one is adopting the response most favoured by the considerations adduced, as is the case in all sound reasoning.[2] So in that respect deductive reasoning, despite its formal validity, is no different from practical reasoning. The main distinctive feature is the explanation of why these things favour the relevant response, which is clearly different from the explanation of the cogency of ordinary practical reasoning. Note, however, that I am able to say this without having yet offered any account of what does in fact explain the cogency of ordinary practical reasoning. (That account, which appeals to the notion of value, will come in 5.4.)

This difference in explanation is not the only way in which formal reasoning differs from ordinary practical reasoning, since we must also admit that intensification and attenuation, enabling and disabling have no role to play in formal deductive reasoning. Here there is no more or less; it is all or nothing. Nor are we likely to come across exclusionary reasons. Maybe some of Toulmin's distinctions apply (the idea of warrant still has application, for instance), but not all.

---

[2] Again, this ignores the possibility of enticing reasons, though perhaps in the theory of reasons for belief there is less room for the enticing.

4.2 Non-Formal Theoretical Reasoning

If we are able to capture a fundamental similarity between practical reasoning, as we have characterized it, and formal reasoning, within the constraints we have imposed (such as that no proposition is capable of favouring a response), our chances of capturing the nature of non-formal theoretical reasoning are surely good. Here the rhetoric of propositions has less currency. But less is not the same as none.

Let us imagine, then, a detective trying to work out who did the dreadful deed, understanding this as an exercise in theoretical reasoning intended to lead to a belief to the effect that N did the deed, for some N yet to be identified. In general there is no difficulty in mapping such an exercise in a grid of the sort that we have used before. There will be a set of considerations, probably quite complicated, and the reasoning will no doubt be various in form. Some considerations will eventually be rejected as misleading or irrelevant. Others will be rejected as simple mistakes. The basic role played by many considerations will be that of raising the probability that N did the deed. The fact that N had a clear motive, for instance, raises that probability; the claim that he was seen some distance away at the relevant period reduces it, unless it itself proves to be a dubious identification—and so on. Will the reasoning then consist entirely of listing considerations that either raise or lower the probability of some 'conclusion'? I doubt it. The issue is a large one because it concerns the claim that relevance in theoretical reasoning consists purely in the raising or lowering of probabilities. I am going to deny that claim, but it is worth pausing to consider what difference it would make to the overall picture that I am trying to promote if that claim were true. So here is a grid:

Belief	N had a strong motive
Belief	N was in the vicinity
Belief	N is the guilty party

We can map the relevant favouring in the familiar way, thus:

Belief	N had a strong motive
Belief *favour*	N was in the vicinity
Belief	N is the guilty party

So certain considerations favour believing N to be the guilty party. Now we ask our explanatory question: what is the explanation of that favouring? In the case of the two considerations mapped above, it is probabilistic. That N had a strong motive makes it more probable that he is the guilty party, and that N was in the vicinity does the same, independently. This makes it appear that probabilification is a relation between certain actual states of affairs and other possible (and perhaps actual) states of affairs. If so, it is a relation between items in the right-hand column of our grid. The ability of the considerations adduced to make a case for believing the conclusion is not explained, as in the formal case, by some structural relation between propositions, but by substantial relations of probabilification. Here then is the full grid:

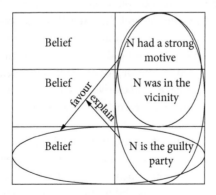

Belief	N had a strong motive
Belief *favour* *explain*	N was in the vicinity
Belief	N is the guilty party

4.3 Belief and Credence

There is another way of approaching these matters, in terms of the raising or lowering of credence. A credence is a mental state which can be increased or reduced, raised or lowered, strengthened or weakened; it is a matter of degree in a way that belief is not. (If there are degrees where belief is concerned, they are probably degrees of confidence, which is something else.) If we are thinking in terms of credences, we can say either that a certain credence is favoured, or that what is favoured is raising one's current credence, or lowering it.

This difference between belief and credences is important, and it would be wrong to think of everything in terms of belief, as I have been doing so far, on the theoretical side (unless we reject the very notion of a credence, which some do, and with some reason). Still, whichever way one goes—that is, whether one is thinking in terms of beliefs or of credences—we still have something that is favoured and something else that is favouring it, and this looks like a relation between the considerations on the right-hand side and whatever we are putting on the bottom line. We don't need to change the basic structures we are familiar with to accommodate talk of credences. It would not be true to say that it is credences that do the favouring, for instance. It may be, however, that the degree to which one's evidence raises the probability of one's conclusion, or favours accepting that conclusion, is affected by the strength of the relevant credence. The credence, on this account, would not be the input to reasoning; that input is the supposed matter of fact in which we have credence. But there is no reasoning (other than toy reasoning) without credence, and the strength of the case made is not 'objective', on a credence-based account, but is sensitive to one's credence in the evidence. And we might need to introduce a distinction between the strength of a reason and the degree of change of credence favoured by that reason. One can have a conclusive reason to raise one's credence a little, or a weak reason to raise one's credence considerably. But I shall ignore this complication in what follows.

Working then in terms of credences, we would still want to know what explains the ability of a consideration to make the relevant difference, that is, to favour a change in credence. Are we forced to return to the idea that there is a relation of probabilification between premises and conclusion, going down the right-hand side? And if we are, should we take ourselves to be discussing a relation of probabilification that obtains between propositions, as that which explains the way in which the considerations adduced favour a change of credence?

My own view about this is that there is nothing wrong with supposing a probabilifying relation going down the right-hand side, but that we should avoid understanding that relation as one that obtains only between propositions, if possible. First, it is only a true proposition, at best, that can make another probable. Second, a probable proposition is one that is probably true; so what we are really dealing with here is the idea that the truth of one proposition can make another proposition more probably true than it was 'before' or would be 'otherwise'. (Of course the 'before' is a bit odd here, since we are not really dealing with temporal relations.)

But third, it is not obvious that 'probable' here must mean 'probably true'. There are probable events, and these might be events whose occurrence is probable, and this need not be identified with there being events of which it is probably true that they will occur. If we can take this sort of line with events, we should be able to take a similar one with states of affairs. States of affairs may be probable in the sense that they are states whose obtaining is probable, rather than states of which it is probably true that they obtain. So just as it is true that 'he will probably come' need not mean that it is probably true that he will come (though no doubt it has that consequence), so 'the cliff is probably friable after last night's rain' need not mean that it is probably true that the cliff is friable, but that the cliff is probably in that state.[3]

Thinking then in those terms, there is no threat to our general approach to reasoning. In reasoning, we present considerations that taken together favour a certain sort of response, and we respond in that light.

---

[3] A. Hayek allows in his entry on probability in the *Stanford Encyclopedia* that the bearers of probabilities are sometimes also called 'events' or 'outcomes', but says the underlying formalism remains the same. Also he points out that subjective probabilities need a ground, and relative frequencies might provide such a ground—but they will need to be understood either as frequencies of events or of states of affairs. Propensities are also features of states of affairs, or of types of physical situation.

4.4 Credence-Changing

This section merely signals a rather different issue, which arises when we try to construct grids for reasoning, not to belief, but to a change in credence. If I reason 'p, q, so r', the grid for belief looks ordinary enough; that p and that q favour believing that r. But how are we to represent considerations that favour raising one's credence that r? We might try:

Believing	p
Believing	q
Raising credence that	r

suitably mapped.

But this would be peculiar, since the friend of credences will be thinking in those terms all the way through, not just at the end. So the grid should look something like this:

Credence > 0.5	p
Credence > 0.5	q
Raising credence that	r

But now suppose that the reasoner already has a high credence that r, and that though someone with a lower credence would be given reason to raise it, all that our believer has is more reason to have his high credence. So the reasons do not really favour his raising his credence at all.

Even for those whose credence that r is lower, and who are here given reason to raise it, the question how much they should raise it might get different answers for different people, in ways that are not yet revealed in the grid. So we cannot represent the bottom left-hand box as 'raising credence to n%', or as 'raising credence by n%'.

We might try to cope with the former difficulty by writing 'raising credence to n% if one is not at that level already'. I am not sure that this is a very satisfactory resolution, but it has the merit of resembling a reason to go to London if one is not there already.

What is more, it might be that the degree of credence one has in the considerations adduced itself affects the extent to which they favour increasing credence in the 'conclusion'. This would be some form of intensification.

All that I have to say on this front is that thinking uniformly in terms of credences introduces considerable complications.

4.5 Beyond Favouring Again

So far I have been talking as if there is only one sort of thing that a consideration can do in theoretical reasoning, only one form of relevance it can have, namely to favour raising or lowering credences or more simply favour belief or disbelief. (Perhaps these make two sorts of thing.) But of course there are other contributions that a consideration can make in theoretical reasoning, just as there are on the practical side. Might not one consideration intensify the degree to which some other consideration favours raising credence appropriately, or favours outright belief? This would be the analogue of the intensification of some other consideration's ability to favour a practical response. An example here might be that nobody else had much of a motive; we could say that this serves to raise the probability that N did the deed, which explains the way it favours increased credence. But it does it, not directly, but by intensifying the extent to which N's obvious motive favours giving high credence to N's being the guilty party—which is achieved, not directly, but by increasing the degree to which N's motive probabilifies his guilt. So again we would see the same sort of structure: the thing or things that are doing the favouring, the response that is favoured, and the explanation of that favouring.

It is quite common for those who think in terms of credences to suppose that one consideration can annihilate (in the sense of reduce to nil) the extent to which another consideration raises one's credence in a conclusion. John Pollock once wrote:

Where P is a prima facie reason for Q, R is a rebutting defeater iff R is a reason for denying Q. All work on non-monotonic logic and defeasible reasoning has recognized the existence of rebutting defeaters, but it has sometimes been overlooked that there are other defeaters too. For instance, 'x looks red' is a prima facie reason for 'x is red'. But if I know not only that x looks red but also that x is illuminated by red lights and red lights can make things look red when they are not, then it is unreasonable for me to infer that x is red. Consequently, 'x is illuminated by red lights and red lights can make things look red when they are not' is a defeater, but it is not a reason for thinking that x is not red, so it is not a rebutting defeater. Instead, it attacks the connection between 'x looks red' and 'x is red', giving us a reason for doubting that x wouldn't look red unless it were red. The preceding indicates that if P is a prima facie reason for Q, then the negation of 'P wouldn't be true unless Q were true' is a defeater. . . . Such defeaters are undercutting defeaters. I have argued elsewhere that rebutting defeaters and undercutting defeaters suffice for describing all defeat relations.   (1994: 379)

In response to this, one might say, first, that a reason for not-Q is not as such a defeater of anything. It only defeats a reason for Q if it is stronger than that reason. Second, and more importantly, a reason R for believing that Q is not in any way dependent on the thought that R would not be the case unless it was the case that Q. So it is not defeated, or even attenuated, by the falsehood of that thought. Only if R is a conclusive reason would it be true that R would not be the case if it were not the case that Q. But we are dealing with prima facie reasons, not conclusive ones (always allowing, what I do not in fact believe, that the notion of a conclusive reason makes sense in the first place). Of a prima facie reason, all one can say is that it counts in favour of believing that Q, or that it raises the probability that Q is true. Further, an undercutter should be a consideration in the presence of which that P does not favour believing that Q at all, or does not raise the probability of Q even a little bit. There may be such things as undercutting defeaters, but Pollock's example is not one. A good example would be one that I have used elsewhere, of a drug that makes red things look blue and blue things look red. That you have taken such a drug means that the fact that a thing looks red to you is no reason to believe it to be red, and is instead a reason to believe it to be blue. But this is a very special case. Third, a reason for believing that P is not itself a reason for disbelieving anything or everything incompatible with P. To support one possibility is not necessarily to diminish the standing of others. My intention to go to Rome tomorrow reduces the probability that I will stay at home, but it does not reduce the probability that I will die during the night.

One might indeed suppose that rebutting and undercutting are the only two forms of defeat; for to defeat a supposed reason R to believe that Q one must either argue that though R does favour believing that Q, believing that not-Q (or not believing that Q?) is more favoured by something else, or argue that R does not favour believing that Q in the first place. But in the latter case what has been shown is that *in this case*

P was not a reason at all. It was not a reason that was undercut and so defeated; it was undercut and so not a reason at all.

Still, the real point here, against Pollock, is that there are three forms of attack, if not defeat. There is being stronger on the other side; there is preventing this one from being a reason in the first place; and there is weakening the support this reason gives, so that (perhaps) some consideration on the other side is now conclusive or at least sufficient. One cannot make the third method simply out of what the other two do, mainly because the second method is not a matter of degree.

4.6 Respecting the Distinction between Intensification and Favouring

To return to our main theme: is it the case that all relations between relevant considerations in theoretical reasoning can be expressed in terms of the raising and lowering of credences? One answer is that intensification and attenuation do take place here as they do with practical reasoning. Even if the only consideration relevant in theoretical reasoning is the probability of truth, the presence of a consideration which itself is not a reason, that is, favours no raising or lowering of credence, can cause some other consideration to favour raising credences more than it otherwise would.

What is more, I have not bound myself to the view that the right way to explain the favouring of changes of credence is always by appeal to the raising and lowering of probabilities. David Bakhurst suggested to me that philosophical argumentation does not seem best characterized always as the attempt to raise the probability of its conclusion. There are other things that we might try to raise or lower, such as plausibility, making sense, and coherence, the latter being understood in terms of relations of mutual explanation. There is no reason why I should not accept, and even welcome, such additions. There is no need for a single or simple answer to these questions about explanation.

One might unwarily suppose that the way in which a case is made is piecemeal, out of independent, free-standing probability-raisers. But this depends upon being able to express every form of relevance within that limitation, and I believe this to be impossible. If E is evidence for B, and G intensifies the degree to which E probabilifies B, then it is true that the combination of E and G raises the probability of B more than E does alone. But to say this (that the combination raises the probability more than either element does alone) is not yet to distinguish the role of an intensifier from that of an independent probability-raiser. The combination of E and G raises the probability of B more than E does alone in two quite distinct situations; the first is where G is an independent reason for the same conclusion (though we should note that adding one independent reason to another does not always strengthen the case), and the second is where G is not an independent reason, but serves merely to increase the extent to which E raises the probability of B. In the latter case there is only one probability-raiser; in the former there are two. One can even imagine a case in which a feature G that would be an independent reason in the absence of E, ceases to be such a reason when combined with E and becomes merely an intensifier of E.

An example of this elaborate sort of possibility might help (but remember that the main point here is the distinction between contributing as an independent reason and contributing by strengthening a reason, which does not itself require the sort of special case I am now trying to illustrate). Here is one about a jazz club that has nightly concerts, which in its essentials I owe to Daniel Muñoz:

H: Tonight's concert will be excellent.
E1:   Miles will be playing at the concert tonight.
E2:   John will be playing at the concert tonight.

The relevant facts are that Miles and John are both fairly likely to give excellent concerts on their own, but they react differently to the stress of playing on the same bill. Miles, it turns out, can't handle the stress of it all, and is likely to perform poorly whenever he's playing on the same bill as John. John, on the other hand, relishes the chance to compete, and is almost certain to excel if playing on the same bill as Miles, in such a way as to increase the probability that the show as a whole will be excellent, despite Miles's failure to shine.

So, we might reasonably assign something like the following probabilities to the ways things could go: $\Pr(H) = 0.25$, $\Pr(H \text{ given } E1) = 0.6$, $\Pr(H \text{ given } E2) = 0.6$, $\Pr(H \text{ given } E1 \wedge E2) = 0.9$.

But in the event that both Miles and John are to play at the concert, only John's presence will contribute in a certain way to the high probability of an excellent evening—though the fact that Miles will be playing will explain why the fact that John will be there makes it so likely that the concert will be excellent—almost certain, in fact. The roles of E1 and E2 in this scenario are different. The likelihood of an excellent show is increased by the presence of E1, but not in the same way as it is by E2, even though E1 would have done so in exactly that way had it not been for the fact that E2.

Now the point of examples like this is not that they *prove* that probabilification is not the only game in town.[4] I think that what they do is rather to show what might be in the mind of those who say that probabilification is not the only game in town, in a way that challenges those who think otherwise to show why their account *must* be right.

4.7 Respecting Complexity

While one is looking for complexities which, even if located within a broadly probabilistic conception of non-deductive reasoning, may themselves be hard to capture in probabilistic terms, here is another example which requires some unpacking. You are a detective investigating the murder of the appallingly proud and domineering Lady Snobgrass. She was shot and you find the gun in the butler's cupboard. Here then, are some relevant considerations:

1. The gun was found in the butler's cupboard.
2. There were no signs of its being a plant (that is, to have been planted there for you to find, so as to cast suspicion on the butler).
3. Your investigation has been conducted with great care.
4. There are no other serious suspects.
5. The butler had something (but not much) of a motive.

Let us consider the respective roles of these 'premises', and start by allowing that the first premise, considered alone, is an independent reason to believe that the butler did the deed. (What the 'considered alone' actually means here is a source of considerable difficulty, but I won't open that can of worms here.) That is, putting the point in terms of belief rather than of credences, it favours believing that the butler did it. The second premise is more interesting. It seems to be

---

[4] The worry about this example is that Miles's presence changes the facts, not the favourings/probabilifications. But of course I have other examples up my sleeve.

relevant, but in what way? Perhaps it intensifies the reason given us by the first premise. But consider how things would have been if the second premise had been false. In that case, the first premise would have favoured believing that the butler was innocent. That is, the falsehood of the second premise would have turned the first premise from a reason to believe the butler to be guilty to a reason to believe him innocent. (It looks like an undercutting defeater.) I take this fact to be part of the relevance of the second premise as it stands. For each premise, we need to consider how things would have been had that premise been false. (Perhaps this is a general rule for those trying to understand how reasoning works.) The first premise is such that if it has been false, we would have had one fewer reason to believe the butler to be guilty. The second premise is such that if it had been false, we would have had one fewer reason to believe the butler guilty, and a very good reason to believe him innocent.

Of course the way I have formulated the second premise is a bit cagey, since it allows for the later realization that the gun was carefully arranged in that way by the butler himself, in an attempt to divert suspicion. But such possibilities are an unavoidable feature of all reasoning of this sort.

What about the third premise? Here the suggestion I want to make is that it is effectively a comment on the reliability of the premises as a whole, though not of the reasoning since it concerns the input to that reasoning rather than what you do with that input once you have got it. So one thing it does is to support the idea that there is not much that you have missed, and this goes beyond any suggestion that the truth of your premises is comparatively solid. There can be other such comments or reminders interspersed in one's reasoning, such as a note that one is not sure about this consideration, or not sure enough to rely on it entirely; there is no reason why one should not lard one's reasoning with such comments, including, for instance, a reference to another similar case.

As for the fourth premise, this seems to me not to be an independent favourer. It would favour believing that the butler did it only if the case against him were strong enough on its own, which it might not be. In a way it is more like a counsel of despair, or perhaps a note of caution. Now we know that we ought not to believe that the butler did it, even if he is the only serious suspect, unless the case against him can be made out sufficiently well. But this is an 'ought', or rather an 'ought not', and tells us little about what reasons we have, where reasons are understood as considerations favouring a certain response. We can perfectly well have some reason to believe the butler did it but not enough to justify coming to that conclusion. There is no principle of detection, or of other enquiry, that one ought to believe whatever one has most reason to believe, if one would do better not to believe anything at all yet.

In addition, the fourth premise depends for its significance on whether we have eliminated all other potential suspects, or whether we just haven't looked very hard.

Finally, the fifth premise. I take this to be an enabler. A strong motive would probably count as a favourer, but a motive of this weak sort seems to do little more than allow the butler to remain under suspicion. It hardly promotes the case for his guilt beyond that.

What is the conclusion from all this? The general point is that theoretical reasoning is very similar to practical reasoning in all the sorts of ways that I outlined in Chapter 3. We could indeed hope to map a detective's reasoning using the tools that have emerged. So to this extent theoretical and practical reasoning are on a par.

There remains, however, the question what relation or relations explain the ability of the considerations adduced to favour the relevant belief—the conclusion. I maintained that in practical reasoning it is not relations between propositions that explain the ability of various considerations, when taken together, to favour this course of action or that. (I did not, however, address the question what does explain this; I do that in 5.4.) But I allowed that in formal deductive reasoning it is relations between propositions that explain why these considerations favour that belief. So how does it stand with non-formal theoretical reasoning? It may yet be, for all that has emerged, that everything here is driven by probabilistic relations, though myself I see reason to doubt that this is so. But if it is, are probabilistic relations to be taken to be relations between propositions? Of course some relations between propositions are probabilistic. If this proposition is true, then that one is probable, that is, probably true—this is a probabilistic relation between propositions. But this does nothing to show that *all* probabilistic relations are relations between propositions. Is it possible, then, as I suggested earlier, that there should be probabilistic relations between matters of fact, or states make another one probable? As we might say, might one state of affairs make another one probable? At the moment I see no reason why not. If a probable proposition is one that is probably true, a probable state of affairs could be one that probably obtains, and a probable event is one that will probably occur or is probably occurring. And if this is possible, the result is that though we *can* understand theoretical reasoning in probabilistic terms, taking the ability of a consideration to favour a certain belief to be explained by relations between propositions, we can equally well understand it as explained by relations between states of affairs.

Perhaps the main reason for doubting this pleasingly flexible conclusion is that propositions differ from states of affairs, and from matters of fact, in being expressible in only one way. A state of affairs can be variably characterized and it is only under a certain description, as one might say, that it favours a certain form of response. We might suppose that propositions cannot be variably characterized in this way.

We could perhaps block this by suggesting that states of affairs have aspects, and the aspects are not multiply characterizable in the way that the states of affairs are. Any variability in characterization of an aspect of a state of affairs will be mirrored by variability in characterization of a proposition.

Appendix: Harman's *Change in View*

Harman begins his book by discerning two distinct subject-matters.

The first is reasoning. Reasoning is something we do, and we do it better or worse. There are principles of reasoning, of two sorts. There are 'maxims of reflection', which tell us what to consider before revising one's view, and there are 'principles of revision', which concern the actual changes to be made. (An example of the latter is that one should try to achieve an equilibrium between minimizing changes to one's view, maximizing its coherence, and managing to achieve a suitable satisfaction of one's ends.)

The second subject-matter is argument and proof. There is a clear difference in category. Argument and proof are not understood as things we do, but as logical structures. Rules of argument are not practical rules, like those of reasoning. Examples of rules of argument are principles of implication, which tell you what implies what—such as *modus ponens*, for example. Such rules are not rules for revising one's view.

Harman's Chapter 2 starts thus:

> Even if they agree that logic is not by itself a theory of reasoning, many people will be inclined to suppose that logic has some sort of special relevance to the theory of reasoning. In this chapter I argue that this inclination should be resisted. It turns out that logic is not of any special relevance.   (1986: 11)

Since I am one of those who suppose that logic is of special relevance to a certain class of reasonings, namely those that aim to achieve the sort of compellingness that comes with formal validity, I need to consider this. My view is that logical canons constitute the explanation of the fact that certain supposed matters of fact (such as that p and that if p then q) favour believing that q. They do this because it is impossible for those two things to be the case without its also being the case that q; and the reason why this is impossible can be revealed by a truth-table.

What does Harman have to say against this? It turns out that what he has to say does not impact on it at all. He starts by saying that if logic does have a special relevance to reasoning, its relevance must be captured at least roughly by two principles, thus:

Logical Implication Principle: The fact that one's view logically implies p can be a reason to accept p.

Logical Inconsistency Principle: Logical inconsistency is to be avoided.

He makes two remarks. The first is that the Logical Implication Principle entails that, if one believes both p and if p then q, that can be a reason to believe q. But, he says, it is not *always* a reason to believe q. Sometimes in such circumstances one ought not to believe q.

But this way of putting things is wrong in two ways. First, it is not one's believing p and that if p then q that is the reason for one to believe q; it is those supposed matters of fact. If they are not the case, one has no reason to believe q, though one will of course mistakenly suppose otherwise. So Harman's first principle is just misconceived. And the explanation of this is that he has failed to see the ambiguity in the phrase 'one's view logically implies q'. He takes it to mean that one's viewing things this way logically implies q. But what it really means is that the things one is viewing, namely that p and that p implies q, logically imply q.

Second, that one ought not to believe q does nothing to show that one had no reason to believe q. But the Logical Implication Principle only spoke of having a reason and says nothing about oughts. Weaker, even: it said only that the fact that one's view logically implies q *can* be a reason.

The main message here is that one can perfectly well hold that logic has a special role to play in the analysis and explanation of certain passages of reasoning, without committing oneself to anything like Harman's first principle. So criticisms of appeals to that principle are irrelevant, even if otherwise correct (which his second criticism is not).

Harman does make a second point that is more telling:

Many trivial things are implied by one's view which it would be worse than pointless to add to what one believes. For example, if one believes p, one's view trivially implies 'either p or q', 'either p or p', 'p and either p or r' and so on. There is no point in cluttering one's mind with all these propositions.   (1986: 12)

Still, if someone does want to know whether 'either p or q' is true, believes that p and reasons from that (from p, that is) to the belief that either p or q, he is not doing something that there is no reason for him to do. There may be little point in doing it, but that is another matter. We are not saying that he should do it.

Another argument, related to me by Sinan Dogramaci but apparently not to be found in this chapter, is that the necessity that binds *modus ponens* cannot be the explanation of how it is that the premises favour believing the conclusion, because there are other cases, much more complex, where the necessity is still there but it is too complicated for us to follow.

But to this one might say that what is being explained is not the person's believing the conclusion, but how it is that the considerations adduced favour the response. If one does not know that they do so, one is not going to respond in the way favoured. But that is irrelevant to my structures.

In the final four pages of his Chapter 2 Harman argues thus:

One might have no reason to accept something that is logically implied by one's beliefs if there is no short and simple argument showing this. To take an extreme example, one accepts basic principles of arithmetic that logically imply some unknown proposition p which is the answer to an unsolved mathematical problem: but one has no reason to believe p if one is not aware that p is implied by these basic principles. This suggests revising the Logical Implication Principle:

Revised Logical Implication Principle One has a reason to believe p if one recognizes that p is logically implied by one's view.

This is a mistake. It is not true that if one is not aware of the considerations that give one good reason to move away fast, there is no good reason to do so. It is only true that one is not aware of that reason. Similarly, if one is aware of the considerations that give one good reason, but not aware that they give one good reason, one still has a reason of which one is not aware. Having a reason is one thing, being aware of it is another. There is no reason to adopt the Revised Logical Implication Principle.

5

Moral Reasoning and the Primacy of the Practical

In this chapter I consider how to locate moral reasoning in terms of the structures that have emerged so far. I am not attempting to write a complete theory of moral thought. My main purpose is rather to reassure myself that moral reasoning—which might seem to be somehow both practical and theoretical at once—can be perfectly well handled using the tools we have developed in previous chapters. I also consider the question how we are to explain practical reasoning—and practical reasons more generally—by contrast with the explanation of theoretical reasons and reasoning offered in Chapter 4. This leads us to the first appearance of the Primacy of the Practical.

5.1 Different Conceptions of Moral Reasoning

So far we have considered the nature of practical reasoning and the nature of theoretical reasoning, both deductive and probabilistic. There remains moral reasoning. Where is this to be located?

One thing we might mean by 'moral reasoning' is reasoning from a moral consideration to action. This is practical reasoning, where one of the considerations adduced is explicitly moral. So one might reason: this would be wrong; still, it would be fun, and nobody will notice, so here goes. Such reasoning is moral—or rather immoral, I suppose. More moral (i.e. more reputable) would be: this is the right thing to do, so—despite the disadvantages—here goes. Of course we should remember here that officially (in 1.1) I have distinguished between acting for a reason and acting in the light of reasoning, with the latter being more complex than the former. So a convincing example of moral reasoning to action needs to be more complex than just 'This is right, so I'll do it'; but perhaps the insertion of the disadvantages—the predictable despite-clauses—will introduce the complexity required.

Obviously this category of reasoning is only as well defined as is the notion of an explicitly moral consideration, and it is notorious that this notion is not well defined. But nothing hangs on that problem at this point; we can safely pass it by. The main point is that this is ordinary reasoning to action (the 'here goes' of the previous paragraph being an attempt to express in words a decision to act, which may simply be the initiation of the action), distinguished only by the fact that one of the considerations adduced has moral content.

But there is something else that we might mean by 'moral reasoning', which does not require the reasoner to reason to action from considerations that are explicitly moral (whatever that amounts to). Such reasoning might still be called moral, if, for instance, acting in that way is made right by the considerations adduced, even though the reasoner does not take note of that in their thought. For someone who reasons as a good person would reason may not be thinking in terms of the right and the wrong at all (or even in more contributory terms of reasons of various sorts), but simply responding to the needs of others (say) as good people do. Such reasoning is moral reasoning in the sense that it is morally reputable.

Take a case of this second sort. Our reputable agent reasons:

| Belief | That guy looks hot, thirsty, and broke; he needs a beer |
| Belief | Though I have to go soon, I can afford to stay for another five minutes and to get him that beer |

and acts accordingly, that is, gets him the beer. This is moral reasoning in the sense that it is reasoning that is morally reputable. It is not made morally reputable by the presence of an explicitly moral 'premise'. It is made morally reputable by being the way (or a way, at least) in which a morally reputable person would reason (and indeed act) in such a circumstance.

So we have two distinct sorts of moral reasoning to action. And then there is, of course, reasoning to moral belief (and presumably there is morally reputable reasoning to belief, but I leave that aside as having been already dealt with). Such reasoning counts as theoretical, simply because it is reasoning to belief. But it might be sensible to bear it in mind, because we want a smooth overall account of moral thought and its relation to action. In what follows we will also need to bear in mind the distinction whose importance emerged in the previous chapter, between such questions as what the considerations are that we are reasoning from and the relations in which they stand to the thing we are reasoning to, on the one hand, and questions about what explains the ability of such considerations to stand in those relations to our 'conclusion' (note the scare quotes), on the other.

5.2 Reasoning to Moral Belief

I start with reasoning to an explicit moral belief. There is of course one picture of this process that is perfectly comprehensible and which would have the consequence that the relation that explains the ability of morally relevant considerations to favour this or that belief about how one ought to act is a relation between propositions. One form of principled ethics has it that we effectively deduce conclusions about how we ought to act from a complex of beliefs that consists of acceptance of a moral principle plus a set of partly non-moral beliefs about the situation that faces us. This will only work if the relevant principle is a principle of the right, what is sometimes called an 'absolute' principle. Absolute principles are of the form 'If an action has feature F, it is right, whatever other features it may have.' Of course 'F' here may be very complex— and it will have to be, if this 'absolutist' picture of moral reasoning is going to work at all. But if we are dealing with an absolute principle, we might hope that there can be a propositional relation that binds our principle, plus a belief that the action would indeed have feature F, to the conclusion that acting in this way is right. If so, the explanation of the ability of the considerations adduced to favour the moral belief will appeal to a propositional structure, namely the form 'All As are Bs; this is an A; so this is a B.'

All this would of course be fine (under the supposition that enough absolute principles can be provided to cover the ground required), if the conclusion of the reasoning were (the belief) that acting in this way would be right. But my own view is that, if one wants to think in terms of reasoning from principles at all (which I myself don't), a 'system' of prima facie (Ross) or pro tanto (Broad) principles is far more promising and plausible as an account of how moral thinking (that is, reasoning to moral belief) actually works than is a system of absolute principles. But with this we lose the supposed advantage of the appeal to absolute principles, namely the possibility of inference to moral conclusions that is grounded in propositional relations, being in its own nature effectively syllogistic. Instead we get a picture of moral thought according to which, as Ross rightly says, one might know all the premises to be true but not be in a position to know the conclusion to be true. And the reasoning is not probabilistic either. It seems therefore that in a Rossian system, the ability of various considerations to favour some particular moral conclusion is not to be explained by appeal to relations between propositions. More probably, the explanation appeals to a grounding relation, which obtains between features of the situation which ground prima facie duties and the rightness of responding in a certain way, that is, a duty proper to act which is grounded in the interaction between those prima facie duties which throws up one of those duties as the most pressing in the present case.

There remains even then an explanatory question to press, namely what explains the ability of the various considerations to ground prima facie duties. Ross does not seem to have addressed that question, perhaps because he saw no prospect of an enlightening general answer. But Prichard does say that 'unless the effect of an action were in some way good, there would be no obligation to produce it' (2002: 2), and I think he would say the same about a prima facie duty or a reason to produce it. I mention this because of what is to follow shortly.

If we don't think there are principles, even of the Rossian type, our reasoning to a moral belief will not be able to have that sort of starting point. Instead, it will start from beliefs about what will upset other people, what might help them—that sort of thing. I might reason: he really would not like me to do this, and has always treated me with kindness; so I ought not to do it. The considerations adduced favour believing that I ought not to do it. What then explains their ability to do that? One answer is: they make it the case that doing that would be wrong. This is the first sign of what I will be calling the Primacy of the Practical, to which I return in 5.5.

5.3 Explaining Practical (Including Moral) Favouring

So much for reasoning to moral belief. What now about moral reasoning to action? Such reasoning comes in two types, one that introduces an explicit 'moral' consideration and one that doesn't. Let us start with reasonings of the second type. These appear to be more or less straightforward, given the general picture that has emerged in previous chapters. Getting him a beer is an action of the sort most favoured by the considerations adduced, and it is done in the light of those considerations. The agent bears in mind certain considerations and then acts accordingly. That doing so is morally praiseworthy is neither here nor there; it plays no role in the account of his reasoning. As far as I can see, there is no mystery (or at any rate no new mystery) about this.

There does, however, remain the explanatory question: what explains the ability of those considerations, taken together, to favour acting in this way? Asking this question reveals something that may have been painfully obvious already. In Chapter 3 I gave an account of what explains the ability of the considerations adduced to favour believing this rather than that, in terms of such notions as probability, plausibility, and coherence. But I have as yet given no analogous account of what explains the ability of considerations adduced to favour acting in one way rather than another. What explains the ability of a consideration to favour a practical response? I certainly need to have an answer to this question.

The best I can offer is that a reason to act is such a reason because it reveals (or at least points us towards) some value that there would be in so acting. And if it is a moral reason, the relevant value will be a moral value.

What alternative answer might we offer, or even consider? Could we suggest that what explains why a certain consideration is a reason to act is some relation between propositions? Even if, as I have already argued, no proposition can favour an action, it is still possible that what explains the ability of the things that do favour the action (considerations, as we are calling them) to do so might be a propositional relation. Those considerations could have a propositional aspect (speaking very vaguely now) and this could be what we appeal to in giving such explanations of favourings as we are capable of.

The most attractive way of getting this story to work is to rely on the fact that any act we have a reason to do, we have a reason to do intentionally. And as an intentional action, it will be, as I have claimed in 1.8, informed by an understanding of what one is doing, and that understanding might be thought capable of having a propositional content, and of giving such content to the action.

Even so, it seems to me very unlikely that the explanation of the fact that my exhaustion gives me a reason to take a break lies in a relation between two propositions, the best candidates for which are 'I am tired' and 'I am taking a break.' One could only take this suggestion seriously if one saw no more promising line to take. But there is a more promising option, namely that the relevant explanation lies is the fact that, given my exhaustion, taking a break will improve my situation. And this is just the appeal to value. Reasons to act in a certain way are considerations that cast so acting in a favourable light, and the explanation of this is that they reveal a value in so acting. Practical reasons for believing will also be of this sort: they will reveal a value in so believing, and this will be a value that is independent of the truth or even the probability of what is believed.

There are two respects in which this attempt to explain the favourings involved in moral reasoning by appeal to value is controversial. These need to be mentioned even if only so as to set them aside. The first is that it would be good to leave room, if possible, for the intuitionist view that the right action need not always be the best, or for the best. Consequentialists tend to understand duty, obligation, and rightness in terms of some (generally maximizing) relation to value. But intuitionists doubt that the connection is as tight as that. They tend to think, with Prichard (1912) and Ross (1930), that where there is duty there will be some value involved, but the relation between the duty and the relevant value will, or at least may, be fairly loose, and certainly won't always be maximization, or even promotion.

The second way in which it is controversial to appeal to value to explain moral reasoning applies to practical reasoning in general, not just to the moral variety. It is that requiring some relation to value seems to amount to taking a stand on the relation between values and reasons and the similar relation between values and obligation (and duty, and rightness). An explanation of reasons by appeal to value rules out one possibility, namely that for something to be of value is just for it to have a feature that gives us some reason to respond favourably to it. This is the so-called 'buck-passing conception of value', which understands value in terms of reasons to respond. Values and reasons will need to be connected less tightly than that if we are to run an explanation of practical reasons in terms of values, because one cannot expect something to explain itself. But this is not the place to address these issues. If no satisfactory resolution of them can be found, this is a general problem, a problem for all rather than just for the views I am presenting here.

5.4 Explicitly Moral Reasoning to Action

I still owe an account of that special class of moral reasonings to action that appeal explicitly to the right or the wrong. The simplest such cases are ones where the train of thought is either 'This would be right; so I'll do it' or 'This would be wrong; so I won't do it.' By this I mean the 'I'll do it' to represent the action, or perhaps the decision, which fits the 'I won't do it' better. But I said in 5.1 that these trains of thought are too simple to count as reasoning; they look more like acting for a simple reason. A more complex case might run: this action has these various features, which overall go to make it wrong; so I won't do it (where this last is the practical decision).

The issue at this stage is not how to explain the ability of the various relevant considerations to favour the response they do. We have already seen how to do that: by appeal to the various values involved. The issue is how to conceive of the relations between the three elements here: right-making features, the rightness made, and the action to be done.

Are we to say that the rightness of an action favours doing it and that the wrongness of an action favours not doing it, or perhaps disfavours doing it? That would certainly be the easiest way forward; it would bring these explicit cases within the scope of what we already have on the table. But the rightness of an action is not an independent favourer. If the action is right, there will be some features that make it right, and which also favour doing it. So are we to say that the rightness made is another favourer, in addition to these? There is some flavour of double-counting here. Or are we somehow to sink the rightness into the successfully right-making features, holding perhaps that these features favour the action in the right-making way or in such a way as to make it right?

There are a lot of rhetorical questions here, but my feeling at this stage is that an enquiry into the nature of reasoning should not be required to answer them all. They really belong to meta-ethics, where for the moment I am going to leave them.

5.5 The Primacy of the Practical (1)

If the reasons for action are such because of some relation to value, how are we to explain the ability of the very same considerations to favour an explicitly moral belief? Suppose that, bearing in mind certain consider-ations, I come to believe that I ought to stop doing what I am doing. What is it that favours my so believing? The answer is by now predict-able. It is the considerations that I have in mind. What explains the ability of those considerations to favour my believing that I ought to stop? The answer is again predictable: it is some relation to value. But it is important that the value concerned will not be the value of believing that I ought to stop; it will be the value of stopping, or perhaps the disvalue of continuing. So it seems that the same considerations, taken in exactly the same way, explain my believing that I ought to stop and my stopping (if I do). But which of these two is primary and which is secondary (if either)? To me it seems natural to suppose that it is because they favour my stopping (and do so in a certain way) that they favour my believing that I ought to stop. That is to say, it is the practical favouring that leads here, and the moral-theoretical favouring that follows. It is not the other way around, that they favour stopping because they favour believing that I ought to stop. This is the first instance of what I call the Primacy of the Practical.

Consider a case where I ought to V: if a consideration is a reason for me to believe that I ought to V, it will normally be (part of) what makes it the case that I ought to V, that is, to play a certain role in making V-ing my duty. There will of course be other reasons to believe that I ought to V, such as the fact that this is what a worthy person would do. This we might think of as a 'secondary' reason, the primary reasons being the features that make the action one that a worthy person would do—that is, the features that a worthy person might have in mind in doing the action, which would not normally include the fact that this is how a worthy person would act. A similar secondary reason might be the fact that one's morally reliable friend has said that this is what one should do, or advised acting in this way. That is certainly a reason to believe that one should do it, and a reason to do it. But it is not a primary reason to act (even if it is a primary reason to believe, which I think possible). The primary reasons to act will be some of the features that were her reasons for saying this—not necessarily all the features that were her reasons, since among those reasons may be such facts as that I am in a muddle, or in need of help, which is not any sort of reason for doing the thing she has advised me to do, even though it is a reason for her to advise me. In general, I suggest that we should be careful not to allow theory to push us towards turning all primary reasons into secondary ones, or more generally to annul or reverse the order of priority here.

5.6 The Primacy of the Practical (2)

These issues all concern our ability to reason to a moral belief. If we want to make sense of moral reasoning to action, and hope to do this by appealing to a propositional relation between the considerations appealed to and the action, we will have to find a 'propositional aspect' of the action, and we have seen some of the problems with this already. The trick is often supposed to be turned by appealing to the intention with which the action is done, finding a propositional aspect for the intention, and then awarding that aspect, vicariously as it were, to the action intended. I have said something about this in Chapter 1, and will be saying a lot more about it in Chapter 9, where I will try to dismantle it. But the main point here is, I think, that even if it were successful in its own terms, it would still not explain what we want explained. The intention is favoured by the relevant considerations, perhaps, but only because the action is. Further, we need to reassure ourselves that 'the intention with which the action is done' picks out an object other than the action itself. But the only way to be sure that this is so is to think of the intention as a 'prior' intention.

And with this restriction, there is some doubt about the notion of a reason to intend. There are certainly reasons to decide to V, reasons to plan to V, and reasons to plan on V-ing; and once one has decided to V, from then on one intends to V. But deciding and planning are actions, and intending to V does not seem to be an action. It is more like a steady state, and though one can have reasons to be in such a state, those reasons will not be the reasons for which one decides to V. A reason to be in such a state is more like a reason to have made up one's mind what to do, and reasons to do that are not likely to be identical with any reasons there may be to act in the way one decides on.

Still, if someone says they intend to V and you ask why, you expect an answer that reveals the desirability of V-ing. With deciding and planning, a reason to decide to V is normally also a reason to V, and the former status depends on the latter in the sense that the reason is a reason to decide to V because it is a reason to V. This is the second instance of the Primacy of the Practical. And if the practical is primary in this way, it seems impossible to explain the practical by appeal to the intentional; it ought to be the other way around.

5.7 Reasons as Evidence

A view that is directly at odds with the Primacy of the Practical is that of Judith Thomson, who understands all reasons, including reasons for action, as facts that are evidence for the proposition that one ought, or ought not, to act (or more generally respond) in the relevant way. This view has the merits of simplicity; that is to say, it simplifies by leaving us with one basic normative concept when one might have thought there were two. (Actually I suppose that in this case we are turning three— reasons, evidence, ought—into two: evidence and ought.) The trouble with simplification, however, is that it is all too easy to oversimplify, and I think this is what Thomson has done.

Thomson's 'General Thesis' is that all reasons-for are reasons for believing (2008: 130), and she understands this as constitutive: to be a reason-for is to be a reason for believing. But this General Thesis is not her overall conclusion; it is merely an intermediate stage on the way to that conclusion. What she is really after is that to be a reason for V-ing is to make some appropriate proposition more probable—to 'lend weight' to that proposition. The intermediate talk of reasons for believing is important for her because she is really working from 'X is a reason to V' to 'X is a reason to believe that one ought to V' and from that to 'X is a consideration that lends weight to the proposition "One ought to V".'

It is worth stressing the strength of Thomson's position here. She is not merely saying that anything that is a reason for V-ing is also some reason to believe that one ought so to V. Many could accept that, and it is not at odds with the Primacy of the Practical. It is something else again to say that *what it is* to be a reason for V-ing is to be a reason to believe that one ought to V.

There is already a problem with this intermediate stage: to be a reason to V is to be a reason to believe that one ought to V. But now suppose we write 'W' for 'believe you ought to V'. The General Thesis seems to require us to say that to be a reason to V is to be a reason to W, and therefore—this is the further claim—to be a reason to believe that you ought to W. But we can then write 'reason to Y' for 'reason to believe that you ought to W'—and so on indefinitely. This is an unhappy result; in my view the regress here is, if not vicious, at least very uncomfortable. It amounts to saying that to be a reason to V is to be a reason to respond in an infinite number of different ways. (Again, note that there would be no problem if the thesis were merely that a reason to V is also, and thereby, a reason to W, and to X, and to Y . . . ; this regress is quite tolerable.)

This regress is avoided if one simply announces, without the intermediate stage, that to be a reason to V is to be a consideration that lends weight to the proposition that one ought to V. So it seems to me that the General Thesis should be quietly forgotten. But this leaves Thomson's central view, that to be a reason to V is to be a consideration that lends weight to the proposition that one ought to V, still standing.

Now Thomson's way of doing things needs to respect the distinction between a reason and an intensifier. An intensifier (in the theoretical realm) is a consideration whose presence is responsible for an increase in the probability of some proposition, but it is only vicariously responsible; the actual probability-raiser is some other consideration, whose probability-raising powers are intensified by the presence of the intensifier. So the notion of evidence as probabilifier needs some fine-tuning here. We have seen all this already.

My first point, however, is that Thomson's account turns secondary reasons into primary ones. A reason to act is being understood as a consideration that stands in a certain relation to a proposition. Now suppose we admit that a reason to V does necessarily stand in that relation to the proposition that one ought to V. We should still remember that it is one thing to say that any consideration that is a reason to V necessarily also plays another role, and a different thing to say that *what it is* for a consideration to play the first role is for it to play the second role. Sometimes Thomson seems to wander on this point, as where she says (2008: 130):

Thus we can of course say, with Scanlon, that for X to be a reason for F is for X to count in favour of F by virtue of lending weight to G, for some G appropriate to F.[1]

If this were her considered view, the remark about lending weight would be Thomson's explanation of how it comes about that X counts in favour of F—an explanation that identifies being a reason with counting in favour. And that is definitely not what Thomson wants to say—which is just as well, I would say, because Thomson's claim that X counts in favour of F 'by virtue of' lending weight to G is to my mind extremely implausible. I would myself take things the other way round and say that X stands in that relation to the proposition G (paradigmatically, that one ought to V) *because* it is a reason to V. It is not a reason to V because it stands in that relation to the proposition that one ought to V, or in virtue of standing in that relation. So the 'becauses' only go one way, and this shows that we are not here dealing with one and the same thing differently described—being a reason to act and raising the probability of the proposition that one ought to act. It is one thing because it is another. The focus of the reason is on acting; that is what it favours. And because it counts in favour of acting, it also makes a contribution to a case for believing that one ought to act. And it does that by making it more probable that one ought to act. So far, nothing has been said against adopting this perfectly natural position, which exemplifies the Primacy of the Practical.

The only argument that Thomson provides for her position on these matters concerns the explanation of reasons. She asks: 'If you think that directive facts [i.e. facts about what you should or ought to do] turn on facts about reasons for action, what do you think facts about reasons for action turn on?' (2008: 156). The succeeding discussion contains a lot of rhetorical questions. One such concerns:

APPLE = the fact that Alice promised Bob that she would give him an apple.

---

[1] F and G in the original are ϕ and ψ.

And Thomson asks what makes APPLE a reason. My answer to this question is that Alice thereby committed herself to giving Bob an apple. Thomson then asks why, once Alice has given Bob an apple, her promise is no longer a reason to give him an apple. But this rhetorical question, which is left hanging, does not seem very hard to me. The answer is that she has already done what her promise committed her to doing.

Another example concerns:

HAT = Bob has just put on a brown hat

And we are asked to suppose that this is a reason for Ann to catch the next plane to Chicago. The question then is why, and various possibilities are mooted, all perfectly sensible. We are then asked what all these alternatives have in common. But first, there need be nothing that all ways in which HAT could be a reason have in common. And, second, it is possible that all such ways are ways in which HAT is related to something of value. My overall conclusion here is that Thomson's arguments for her position, such as they are, are not very persuasive.

Not only do I see no reason to go along with Thomson on these points. I see some reason not to. My worry applies to all views that understand the contribution of an individual reason in terms of overall oughts. It is odd to think that each contributory reason makes some sort of claim about how the balance of reasons will turn out. I would have supposed that an individual reason could be quite a modest affair and make no claim about what other reasons there might be to consider and their individual or cumulative strength.[2]

We might admit that if a consideration is a reason, then if there is no other reason this consideration will be conclusive (where to be conclusive is to ground an ought).[3] But this does not show that the contribution of a reason is itself to be understood in terms of probabilifying an ought, or of lending weight to an ought-proposition.

Let us now return to the explanation of moral belief. Suppose that these considerations favour believing that one ought to stop. What explains their favouring this belief? An obvious answer would be that these considerations are the ones that make it the case that one ought to

---

[2] This point is relevant to the very similar views expressed by Kearns and Star (2009).

[3] Raz (2011: 45–6) denies this claim of theoretical reasons, though he accepts it of practical reasons.

stop; they are right-makers. But not all favourers are right-makers. Favouring is a contributory matter, while right-making takes place at the overall level. So a better answer is just that these considerations make something of a case in favour of stopping. But this is just the Primacy of the Practical. The considerations make something of a case for believing that one ought to stop because they make something of a case for stopping. What explains their ability to make a case for stopping? Answer: some relation to value.

5.8 Three Relations

It seems to me important to distinguish between three relations which one often finds being conflated with each other. There is the relation of 'making right', right-making (often also called ought-making). There is the relation of being a reason to V, a strong form of which is the relation of being a conclusive reason to V. And there is the relation of being a reason to believe it right to V; this is an epistemic reason, officially. We need to keep these separate if we are not to get confused.

It is not very hard to keep the epistemic reason separate from the other two, despite Thomson's efforts to persuade us otherwise. The obvious difference is in focus; the right-making relation and the reason-relation aim at action, and the epistemic reason aims at belief. Still, despite this difference, it is possible for a consideration to play one role because it plays the other—to aim also at action because it aims at belief, and in virtue of that aim, or to aim also at belief because it aims at action and in virtue of *that* aim. The view that I propounded in the previous section had it that a reason for V-ing is, in virtue of that, also a (contributory) reason to believe that one ought to V. But one might worry that this is too strong. There is after all the possibility of enticing reasons; if such exist, they are counter-examples to this general claim. A reason to spend the afternoon fishing is not any sort of reason to believe that one ought to do so. Still, one can imagine a weaker version of the claim, which holds that every practical reason has an epistemic shadow of some sort, stronger or weaker as the case may be.

Let this be so. That leaves us with the relation between right-making and being a reason. Now of course not every consideration that is a reason for action is one that makes the action right, or makes it what we ought to do. We are dealing with contributory reasons here, and only some of those will succeed in right-making or ought-making. This is so even if we restrict ourselves to moral reasons (and the enticing ones won't ever succeed in right-making anyway; that was not their focus). Defeated moral reasons for V-ing do not succeed in making V-ing right. There is, however, a conception of would-be right-making, and we might suppose that any moral reason does that; moral reasons for V-ing, we might say, are would-be right-makers, though they may not succeed in right-making. If they don't, there are three possible explanations. The first is that there are stronger moral reasons for doing something else; the second is that there are equally strong moral reasons against V-ing, or for doing something else. The third is that there are moral reasons against V-ing, so that the case made by the original reasons for V-ing is not strong enough to make V-ing morally required. (Not everyone would agree that this last is possible.)

But if moral reasons are would-be right-makers, and sometimes succeed in making something right, but sometimes fail, we should distinguish any right-making relation from any reason-relation. Reasons-relations are relations of favouring, and I have already laid out the structure of the favouring relation (in 2.5). It is a tripartite structure (at least), having places for the individual consideration that favours, the response that is favoured, and the person who is to respond in that way. Right-making is a completely different form of relation. It is (normally) a relation between several considerations and the rightness that they make together. (It is a success notion.) This is an instance of a more general making-relation, one in which what is made is rightness, as opposed to (say) wrongness, or confusingness, or funniness, or attractiveness. All these features stand on the right hand of a making-relation. This making-relation is a metaphysical relation, not particularly a normative one. (Makers are nothing more than grounds.) The normativity belongs entirely to what is made, not to the making of it, which is a quite ordinary phenomenon.

The reason why people forget to distinguish the reasons-relation (favouring) from the right-making relation is that the same consideration can stand on the left-hand side in each case. A consideration that is a reason for A to V is one that makes right A's V-ing, that is, makes it right for A to V (or at least can do so, and will do so if it is strong enough to stand alone). (So there is a sense, too, in which the action is 'on the right-hand side of the relation', but it is a different sense.) The crucial point here is that, though what favours is also what makes right, and what is made right is also what is favoured, the making in making right is a quite different sort of relation from that of favouring. Favouring is a normative relation, and making is not.

A good example of someone who seems to me to err on this point is John Broome (2004). Broome wants to understand both right-making (equivalently, ought-making) and favouring in terms of contributions to what he calls a weighing explanation of an overall 'ought'—the ought that is made. The main oddity of this is the idea that favouring could *be* an explanatory relation; there is no difficulty in supposing that, by favouring a certain response, a consideration makes a contribution to an explanation of some sort—to an explanation, say, of such case as can be made for acting in the relevant way. It contributes to that explanation by contributing to the thing explained. But Broome supposes that *what it is* to favour—to call for a certain response—is just to be part of an explanation of the rightness of that response, and this seems to me to obliterate the normativity of 'calling-for', which is one way of capturing the normativity of a reason. The essential point is that Broomean reasons are not normative, because everything is understood in terms of a contribution to the explanation of something normative; the normativity of the thing to be explained does not make the elements of that explanation normative in any way.[4]

---

[4] I say more on this topic in my (2015).

6

Taking Stock

In this chapter I consider some general issues about the nature of the account I have been constructing.

6.1 Overview

The position that has emerged after four chapters on practical, theoretical, and moral reasoning is as follows. Reasoning is a process in which we try to work out how to respond to the situation which confronts us. The reasoning is intended to determine the shape of that situation, in doing which we determine what sort of response is most appropriate. When things go at their best, the response adopted is of the sort most favoured in the situation, taken as a whole. Responses can be practical or theoretical. A practical response is an action of the sort most favoured, a theoretical response is a belief of the sort most favoured. Reasoning can take us to either form of response, and can do so directly. We do not need to pass through a theoretical response to get to a practical one, and we do not need to pass through a practical response to get to a theoretical one.

The real difference between practical and theoretical reasoning lies in matters to do with explanation: that is, in the relation that explains the ability of the considerations adduced (at least, of those that are doing the favouring) to favour the relevant response. As I have presented the matter, in the practical case it is what one might call considerations of value that play this explanatory role. In the theoretical case it is truth-relations or relations of probabilification, centrally, with two qualifications. First, the extent to which one consideration raises the probability of a belief (that is, of a thing believed or to be believed) can be affected by the presence or absence of other considerations that affect its ability to play that probability-raising role. Second, it may be that not all theoretical reasoning is driven by relations of probabilification. There are other theoretical desiderata such as coherence and explanatory power. Then in the moral-theoretical it is relations of value that play the basic explanatory role, because of the Primacy of the Practical.

6.2 Is Truth a Value?

It may seem awkward that I have given one form of explanation for theoretical reasoning, and another for moral-theoretical reasoning, reasoning to a moral belief. This awkwardness would be removed, and a desirable unification achieved, if we could understand truth and/or probability as themselves values, as being of value. This would not obliterate the distinction between practical and theoretical reasoning, but it would make them more smoothly similar to each other than I have so far been allowing—which I would take to be an advantage for my general programme. I think that the programme could survive without this advantage, for after all, if there are significant basic differences between practical and theoretical reasons, that is just how it is; we will simply have to put up with it, and my picture can certainly accommodate it. What is more significant is that there is a serious argument of Joseph Raz's that, at least in the case of truth, this assimilation cannot be got to work: truth is not a value. Raz writes:

Imagine... that in all cases, if we have a belief about a certain matter, then it is *pro tanto* better to have a true rather than a false belief, just because it is true. Consider an example: a month ahead of time I believe that Red Rod will win the Derby... There may be ways to increase the likelihood that my belief is true. Perhaps I could give valuable advice to Red Rod's jockey... Is the fact that that will make it more likely that my belief is true a reason to do so? If there is value in one's beliefs being true as such then there should be no difference between making reality conform to the belief and making the belief conform to how things are. (2011: 45)

Raz's final sentence here needs a small qualification. His point is that if truth is itself valuable, it should not matter *to that value* how one gets it, though it may of course matter in other ways. If I believe that I am the best double-bass player in Oxford, and make that true by incapacitating all my rivals, I would still have had a truth-related reason to do that—if being true is a way of being valuable. So Raz's point is that there is no such reason to adjust the world to make one's belief true.

This argument is powerful but, I think, unsuccessful. Against it stands the holistic thought that whether something is of value can depend on context. So here the idea would be that whether the truth of a belief is of value can depend partly on extrinsic factors, such as how it came about that the belief hit the mark. Because of the way one's belief has come to be true, it might lose the value it would have had if it had come to be true in another way; and despite this the relevant value could still be intrinsic. Intrinsic value is not the same as unconditional value. So perhaps Raz's argument can be evaded.

But we should be careful about simply awarding ourselves the prize here. Even if the holistic thought about the variability of intrinsic value is available to us, we should not simply assume that it is correctly applied to the present case. It is not entirely clear how we are to assess the issue, but the question seems to be: would our true belief be deprived of a value it would otherwise have had, by our having so arranged things that it came out true? If it would, we could say that a true belief has value just in virtue of its truth, where it has not been deprived of that value by some extraneous feature of this sort (or in some other unsuitable way); and thus evade Raz's argument. It has value to lose, and it can lose it.

What does it mean to say that truth is a value? One answer is that a belief is always the better for being true. This is not interesting if the sort of value involved is instrumental; there is no doubt that it is at least generally better to have true beliefs than false ones. The idea we should be trying to make sense of is the idea that a true belief has some kind of non-instrumental value, which means, on this account, that it is always the better non-instrumentally for being true. But Raz has given us an example of a belief that is not the better for being true, because of the way in which its truth was achieved. so I hope that we can find a different account of what it is for truth to be a value than the 'always the better for being true' account. (Of course all this is compatible with its being sometimes better overall to be wrong.) Still, I am just raising a warning flag here, and with that caveat I think we can rest content with the idea that truth is a value. The issues that have emerged here just show that the theory of value is not yet in a very good state, as far as these issues go.

Raz has more to say about differences between practical and theoretical reasons. A second point is that practical reasons speak to many concerns and many values, while at best theoretical reasons would speak to one and the same value—the value of truth. Whether this is so or not does not matter to my project. And he has a third point about the fact that one can suspend belief but not suspend action: with belief there is believing, disbelieving, and doing neither, but with action there is no such *tertium quid*; one either does it or does not do it. This is a common observation, though I wonder if there might not in fact be the *tertium quid* of avoiding doing it, analogous to disbelieving; Raz mentions this possibility in a footnote (2011: 46 n. 25) and I would wish to make more of it than he does there. But I leave all these issues aside.

6.3   Is Probability a Value?

What then of moral-theoretical reasoning? This is officially theoretical, and so it should be covered by what has been said about theoretical reasoning more generally. But as I have presented the matter, reasoning to a moral belief is not driven by considerations of probability—or not normally so, at any rate—but by considerations of values other than the value of truth, values belonging to outcomes and actions. (Remember that I have already admitted that I do not know how to characterize the special nature of those values that make a reason moral rather than ordinary-practical.) This was an instance of the Primacy of the Practical. The considerations that favour this course of action, or go to make this course of action the right one, will also, and thereby, favour believing it to be right (in suitable cases). So the explanation of the ability of those considerations, taken in their context, to favour the relevant moral belief appeals eventually not to the way in which they raise the probability that the belief is true, or stand in some other relation to the value of truth (though they will do that too), but to the way in which they favour a practical response.

Still, one might say, even though considerations of probability are not at the bottom of the explanatory tree, they are in there somewhere. We have decided, *contra* Raz, that truth might be a value. What about probability? Could that be a value too? If it were, it would be a rather different sort of value from that of truth. One can imagine thinking that anything that is true is the better for being so (though I suggested just above that this is not as true as we might have hoped). A true friend, a true story, a true hypothesis—there doesn't seem to be any difference on this score. (Can one have a true enemy?) But with probability it is different. It may be that a probable belief is (pretty much?) always the better for being probable, and the same goes for a probable hypothesis. But a probable outcome does not seem to be the more valuable for being probable; indeed, the probability of an undesirable outcome seems to make things worse rather than better. That fact might be thought irrelevant; the outcome doesn't get any the worse for being probable, what gets worse is our predicament as a whole. And even if it did, this would not prevent other things that are probable from being the better for their probability. And there is a further element of variability to be borne in mind. An elegant outfit is the better for being elegant, so elegance is a value; yet an undeserved but elegant insult is, most probably, the worse for being elegant. So the fact that being F is a value is not inconsistent with something's being the worse for being F.

The other way in which we might come to think of probability in evaluative terms is to think of it as a normative notion, perhaps as 'to be believed' or 'to be expected'. This would make probability analogous to such notions as desirability and respectability (and to a gerundive in Latin, of which a classic example is 'Amanda' meaning 'fit to be loved'). The desirable is not just what one can desire, but what is to be desired; the respectable is what is to be respected; perhaps a probable event is one that is to be expected, or that there is reason to expect.

To sum up: there are two distinct ways of coming to think of probability as a value. The first is to announce that probability is itself valuable, or at least can be. The second is to announce that the notion of probability is normative. (To see the potential differences between these two, note that many things that are not normative are still of value, e.g. not being entangled in barbed wire.)

I don't feel in a position to pronounce on this issue either. All I can do is to raise the possibility of a conciliatory position, a *rapprochement*, which first distinguishes firmly between practical and theoretical reasoning and then pulls back a bit, understanding the theoretical side in terms of its own, theoretical, values.

6.4 Raz on Appropriateness

There is still a question whether my picture is stable. Reasoning to a moral belief is officially theoretical, and one might have supposed that it should be treated in the same way as other theoretical reasoning, but I am treating it as grounded in the practical. Is there something unacceptably hybrid about this arrangement? Moral belief is belief. Reasons for a belief should be reasons for supposing the relevant thing believed to be true. Now let us go back to the account that Raz offered us of reasons for belief and reasons for action. On this account, reasons for action are grounded in concerns and values, and reasons for belief are truth-related and not grounded either in the value of believing accordingly or in the value of truth; they are, in Raz's novel terminology, adaptive. He writes: 'Reasons are adaptive if they mark the appropriateness of an attitude in the agent independently of the value of having that attitude, its appropriateness to the way things are' (2011: 47).

Note that this sort of appropriateness can be achieved in more than one way. A true belief is appropriate because of its truth; a reasonable emotion is appropriate in some other way. Anger is an appropriate response to an insult, and this is not—or not necessarily—because there is something good about being angry in that context.

There are two aspects of Raz's official account of the adaptive that we should pay attention to. The first is the notion of appropriateness. This is clearly a normative notion, one that introduces some conception of value. The other is the phrase 'independently of the value of having that attitude'. This qualification is exactly right. If we want to give an account of epistemic/theoretical reasons in terms of epistemic/theoretical values, we should remember that those values are not likely to be values of believing, but values to which believing is properly responsive.[1] But I am not so sure about Raz's gloss on the notion of appropriateness: 'appropriate to the way things are'. This seems to take us back to a non-normative conception of appropriateness, that of a simple match. Matching may be of value, but it is not a value.

Now Raz allows that some reasons for belief are practical, in the sense that they are considerations that establish that so believing has a certain value. If I offer to pay you a million dollars if you manage to believe that you are transcendentally glorious, you have strong reason to do this if you can. But your reason in this case is not adaptive; it is practical. In such cases we are dealing with a belief for which there might also be adaptive reasons (in this case, let us allow, there are evidently not); the practical reason is in addition to those, and operates differently from

---

[1] Here I acknowledge and respond to welcome pressure from Kurt Sylvan.

them. So such cases are not really the ones at issue when we are dealing with moral belief. With moral belief, we have to deal with reasons for believing that one ought to act, as well as with the (moral) reasons for so acting. The reasons for moral belief will be in Raz's terms adaptive, since though they are value-related they are not grounded in the value of so believing; but, I maintain, they will be explained by practical reasons, reasons for doing the thing that one adaptively believes that one ought to do. What makes the belief appropriate is that it is true (we are supposing), and it is made true by the considerations that together call for us to act in that way.

I suggest, then, that this fairly complex account is perfectly stable. It is true that moral-theoretical reasons are adaptive, but this does not prevent them being explained by considerations of value, so long as the value lies not in the attitude we adopt, the believing, but in the nature of (or other aspects of) the action which we correctly judge to be right.

The point, however, is that much the same can be said about theoretical reasoning. There are values to which such reasoning is responsive, but they are not the values of believing as we do.

There will still be cases of moral-theoretical reasoning which are not practical at all. I have already alluded to some examples of these. That a reliable adviser has recommended a certain course of action to me is a reason for me to believe that course of action to be right, but it is not itself among the considerations that make that action right, or among those that make her recommendation correct. Here I have a reason for belief that is merely adaptive. But this is clearly a special case, and our account correctly locates it as such.

6.5 Focalism

Robert Audi offers three arguments against the sort of view I have been developing in this book. He writes:

Granted, the action-as-conclusion view has the virtue of closing the gap between practical reasoning and the action it indicates—by making the action itself the concluding element. This implication may indeed be the chief attraction of the view. But the view has serious defects. It makes practical reasoning a hybrid process composed of what is, intuitively, reasoning and, on the other hand, action based on it. It leaves us with no adequate account of the concluding of that reasoning. And it fails to accommodate cases in which the action that should be the concluding element does not occur.   (2006: 90–1)

What interests me here is the third point. It is merely one instance of a common complaint against positions of the sort I have been trying to build up. The general thrust is that practical reasoning can be interrupted. The reasoner can be distracted, forgetful, prevented, or unaware that the moment has come, or in some other way fail to carry through from deliberation to action. In such cases we would not say that no deliberation has occurred, nor that there is some defect in that deliberation. It was fine as far as it went; the defect lies in the follow-up, or lack of it.

It is noticeable that the same train of thought is not often applied to theoretical reasoning, which as far as I can see is subject to the same defects. Audi does not suggest that the conclusion of theoretical reasoning is only 'I ought to believe such-and-such', on the grounds that sometimes the reasoner is interrupted, prevented, or otherwise distracted from completing what she is about. And he is wise not to do so. For even the 'I ought to believe' conclusion is subject to the same difficulties.

Leaving that rebuttal aside, however (without wanting to minimize the importance I attach to it), I want to suggest in addition that the *form* of Audi's argument is challengeable, in two respects. My first point is that an incomplete instance of something is still an instance of that thing. An incomplete house is still a house—just not a complete one. Of course there is a point in the building before which we would not think that we have here an incomplete house; but after a while the phrase 'incomplete house' seems exactly right for the stage we have reached. The same applies to an incomplete philosophical article. The fact that the final paragraph has not yet been written or the references sorted out does not mean that what we already have is not an article. And a car without one wheel is still a car. These things are described in terms of what they may, or should become. More generally: a defective or merely less than perfect instance of a type does not for that reason cease to be an instance of that type at all.

My second point challenges the idea that any enquiry into the nature of practical reasoning is aiming at providing necessary and sufficient conditions for reasoning of that sort to occur. The Aristotelian thinks that action is part of the reasoning. Still, Audi claims, when someone reasons practically and fails to act accordingly, there may yet be something worth calling reasoning here despite its not including the relevant action. So practical reasoning does not itself include the performance of the relevant action. Something has happened as a result of the reasoning, certainly; perhaps that something is the drawing of an intermediate conclusion about how one ought to act (and this is Audi's own account of how practical reasoning works). But such cases cannot be instances of practical reasoning, on the Aristotelian view, because it has to see them as lacking something whose presence is necessary if they are to count as such. Audi's view, by contrast, is that they are complete instances of something, and that something is what he calls practical reasoning, but they are not complete instances of practical reasoning in the Aristotelian sense. In short: since sometimes the 'right' action fails to be done, but still the reasoning is complete, the conclusion of practical reasoning cannot be an action. The best view therefore is to think of the conclusion of practical reasoning as a judgement (which for him is not yet a belief) on a practical topic, for example about what one ought to do.

This imposes a certain aim on our enquiry, an aim which I take to be optional, and which I do not have. In fact I suppose that that aim cannot be achieved, and that this is not to be mourned. My aim is to come to an understanding of practical reasoning by giving an account of certain instances, carefully chosen for the purpose, and offering to understand other putative cases in the light of those. I think of this as a *focalist* programme. That programme amounts to saying: these things are practical reasoning, and anything sufficiently relevantly similar to them is practical reasoning too, even though it be defective in some way. (I owe everything of interest in this section to discussion with Daniel Wodak, to whom I owe even the term 'focalism'.)

Applying this to the case at hand: I give an account of certain examples, passages of thought that do lead smoothly to action. I then allow that there can be defective instances that are still of the same general type, and which count as instances of that type because of substantial and relevant similarities to the cases that I started from.

One significant sign of focalism is that a focalist is not concerned to give necessary and sufficient conditions for relevant similarity to the focal cases. Focalists leave that up to judgement, and don't much care where the dividing line comes. But they hold that this insouciance does not prevent them from making significant progress in the understanding of the phenomena that concern them.

Instances of focalism can be found elsewhere in philosophy; Daniel Wodak suggested to me that John Finnis's conception of law is a focalist one. Formally, one might say, they tend to involve three moves. First, we identify certain cases as focal; to cover the ground, we probably need a range of cases. Second, we determine a similarity relation between the focal cases and any peripheral cases. Third, we identify a dependence relation that holds between the focal and the peripheral cases.

My own brand of focalism, or at least the sort of focalism I think of as instantiated in my approach to practical reasoning, is of this general nature. I give an account of certain successful cases of practical reasoning, and identify other processes as reasoning, or as practical reasoning, to the extent that, and because, they are relevantly similar to my focal cases. The complex nature of the relevant similarity is given by the material theory of Chapter 3; the 'because' in the previous sentence indicates the dependence relation introduced in the previous paragraph.

My focal cases are cases of ideal reasoning, because they involve no mistake or lapse of any sort. But even then there may be a range of such cases; for a full account, we would need to be sure that we start from a sufficiently wide range to ensure that our account spreads out to cover all the non-ideal cases we want to cover. They will all be sufficiently similar to a focal case to count as reasoning. So though I may allow that a case where someone reasons from considerations that, unknown to her, are not the case, may still be practical reasoning, still I recognize the theoretical primacy of examples where there is no such error. But I may also decide that where someone completely mistakes the practical relevance of the true considerations she adduces, she is not doing something sufficiently similar to a focal case to count as a practical reasoner. There is a limit to one's theoretical tolerance.

So focalism enables us to be unmoved by the worries that so plagued the early part of Paul Grice's *Aspects of Reason* (2001), where the supposedly serious problem was that accounts that start by thinking about entirely successful reasoning (with true premises and a valid form) fail to allow that less successful cases were reasoning at all. But if we broaden our account so as to explicitly include the less successful cases, we will open a door to even more outlandish cases—a door which we will be unable to shut.

Focalism also enables us to deal with certain rather different supposed counter-examples to the account of reasoning that I have been developing here. One such is supposititious reasoning, where someone reasons from things he merely supposes to be true, in order to see what follows from them. This can easily be understood as a sort of play version of the real thing. Instead of signing up to the considerations he is reasoning from, he reasons as if they were the case. And since he is not reasoning from things he believes, what he determines is only the response that would be favoured by those considerations, were they the case. Not surprisingly then, he does not respond in that way.

Another potential counter-example is *reductio ad absurdum*. We reason to the falsehood of some suggestion by supposing it to be true and then deriving its contradictory by means of added premises taken to be true for the purpose. Our thought is: these things, together with the supposition that *p*, favour believing that not-*p*. So we respond appropriately. But this is no counter-example. If a group of considerations, taken together, favour believing a specific one of those considerations not to be the case, we have to adjust somehow, and if we are unwilling to adjust elsewhere, we will know how to identify the culprit.

Focalism is an interesting and understudied methodology. I first came across it (but not by that name) in a conversation with Richard Wollheim long ago. He suggested that, though we may prove to be unable to produce necessary and sufficient conditions for something to be a work of art, we might still make progress by giving detailed descriptions of certain well-chosen instances (and we need a sufficient range of these to cover the ground). Though I don't think he actually drew this conclusion explicitly, still the thrust of his remarks could be that, having done that groundwork, we can announce that anything sufficiently relevantly similar to those instances is also a work of art. There would be no suggestion in this that there is what one might call an algorithm available, one that can be operated without a suitable sensibility to relevant similarities. Such an algorithm would be provided by a standard (i.e. non-focalist) account in terms of conditions for the application of a concept that are individually necessary and jointly sufficient, in the traditional form.

Now we might say that a focalist account does really offer necessary and sufficient conditions of its own, in the sense that, for example, it is both necessary and sufficient for something to be a work of art that it be sufficiently relevantly similar to some of those we have already described. But this is not how necessary and sufficient conditions are standardly conceived. And, more importantly, it distorts the focalist programme to say that in its own way it offers necessary and sufficient conditions. The flexibility of focalism gets lost, conceived in that way. For our list of focal cases can always be expanded, and the discovery that this needs to be done does not do the same damage to the account amended as is done by a counter-example to a set of necessary and sufficient conditions.

Still, a great deal of philosophy involves the search for accounts of that standard necessary-and-sufficient-conditions sort. Take a very different area: the philosophy of action. What is an action? We might say that an action is a bodily movement caused by certain specified combinations of beliefs and desires. Having said this, we get counter-examples thrown at us; some actions are not bodily movements at all (reciting a poem to oneself, perhaps), and some bodily movements caused in the supposedly required way are not actions. We are not allowed just to say that these peripheral counter-examples are not actions because they are not sufficiently relevantly similar to the central ones. Agent-causalists who say that an action is the causing of a change by an agent face the same sort of challenge.

Another interesting question is whether the difference between focal and peripheral cases is always normative—as where the focal cases involve no mistake (e.g. no mistake about relevance, when we are talking about practical reasoning). I do think in this way of my focal examples. And the focal cases that Wollheim had in mind were probably instances of good art, not just good instances of art. But a badly made car is still a perfectly good example of a car.

Note that focalism should not be thought of as offering paradigm cases. Even if there is such a thing as a paradigm case of practical reasoning, it is not important to focalism that its instances be seen as perfect instances. Even if the focal cases are cases where there is no mistake, it might be that some are better than others—in terms of richness, for instance.

7

Instrumental and Other
Forms of Reasoning

In this chapter I consider various ways of capturing the nature and force
of instrumental reasoning, normally understood as reasoning to a necessary means to an already existing end. I give my own account, which,
I argue, is much more flexible than others, to its advantage. I then
consider various problems which my account faces in making sense of
the appeal to one's end in such reasoning, and more generally of the role
of autobiographical considerations (I believe that p, my aim is to V,
I hope/fear that p, etc.) in reasoning.

7.1 Is All Practical Reasoning Instrumental?

Instrumental reasoning is the attempt to work out means by which to
achieve our ends, the ends being supposedly established in advance. By
an 'end' I mean something we are already aiming at, or pursuing—an
aim, one might say. Some writers suppose that instrumental reasoning is
all there is to practical reasoning. In extreme cases they don't even bother
to argue for this.[1] On the other side, there is a beautiful argument by
Sebastian Rödl to the effect that instrumental reasoning cannot be the
sole form of practical reasoning, because the same form of reasoning that
is involved in the selection of the means is involved in the prior selection
of the end (2007: 24–5). My own view is less trenchant: that whether it is
or is not possible for it to be the only form, it is not in fact the only form.

---

[1] An example is Hornsby: 'Practical reasoning, which is reasoning that moves from ends
to means, is prospective reasoning. Starting from an end, it delivers the knowledge someone
has when she is in a position to move towards it' (2013: 14). Note that she does *not* say here
that the means is a necessary means.

But in thinking that all practical reasoning involves the search for acceptable means to our ends, one is committed to two views, both of which I reject. The first view is that there can be no reasoning about ends; we can reason from our ends but not to them. This view is primarily associated with Hume. I take an anti-Humean view, which I am not going to argue for here: that reason alone can lead us to adopt an end. I reject both the Humean view that our ends are generated by desire, by wantings, and the derived (second) view that, since reason cannot deliver ends, all that it can do is to seek out means to ends delivered to it by desire (or passion, as Hume puts it). My view is that it can do that, but it can do more.

By taking this position I give myself problems, as we will see. But quite apart from that, we all agree that there is such a thing as instrumental reasoning, and the question is how to understand the way it works.

7.2 Harman on Practical Reasoning

Gilbert Harman starts his chapter on practical reasoning thus: 'I under-stand practical reasoning to be the reasoned revision of intentions' (1986: 77). This is in line with his general thesis that reasoning is all about whether and how to change one's view (1986: 2). Such views changed may be practical or theoretical. A practical view is a plan, a desire, or an intention; a theoretical view is a belief. We reason from our beliefs, plans, desires, and intentions to new plans, beliefs, or intentions, or to the abandonment of old ones. Either way, in order to change one's view one must first have a view, it would seem.

It is certainly true that we do this, even if it is not the only thing we do. However, Harman makes it appear that all reasoning, practical or theoretical, starts from things to do with the reasoner: 'I believe that p', 'my present plan is to V'—and so on. The reasoner is reasoning not from the view he has (what he believes or intends) but from his having it. An argument for this might be that reasoning has to start from something, and from something that the reasoner is already committed to; otherwise, how could one reason from it? Well, that is true enough—though it seems to me that one could perhaps start from something one suspects or hopes to be true rather than already believes to be true, so long as one is willing to treat it as something to reason from. (I consider how to cope with this sort of possibility in 7.9 below.) Still, to the extent to which it is true, it does nothing to make us suppose that all or any of our 'premises' *must* be of this autobiographical sort. The Head of Department (from the example discussed in 3.9) is faced with a problem. His problem is that he does not have a view about how to proceed and he needs to get one. There are things in the light of which he engages in reasoning, true enough, but it would be wrong to lump them all together so that the supposed matter of fact from which he is reasoning (that his colleague plagiarized his student's work) comes in the same category as a plan or intention of his own. More realistic would be to say that he has (or appears to have) a problem and he needs a solution, but he is not reasoning from his need for a solution, nor from his having a problem. The *aim* of practical reasoning, the aim of a practical reasoner, need not always be to find a means to a given end.

7.3 Is There a Logic of Practical Reasoning?

One of the attractions of the view that all practical reasoning is instrumental is that it makes it at least conceivable that there is a logic of practical reasoning. This is because of the attractions of the idea that instrumental reasoning has a certain logical form.

Very generally speaking, all instrumental reasoning has a form; there are two main forms, reasoning to a sufficient means and reasoning to a necessary means.

But these are merely the two *main* forms; it should not be forgotten that there is also such a thing as reasoning to a partial means. My end is to get to Edinburgh by the end of the day; so I start by driving to Birmingham and seeing how I get on from there, perhaps by catching a train. Getting to Birmingham is neither sufficient nor necessary for the achievement of my end. I could perfectly well have driven to Leeds instead. I mention this often ignored possibility now; it is perfectly consistent with Jennifer Hornsby's remark that 'practical reasoning ... delivers the knowledge someone has when she is in a position to move towards' an end she has, which is a much more flexible conception than most; and I will return to it at the end of the next section, once I have given my own account of reasoning that is to do with necessary and with sufficient means. Any theory of instrumental reasoning needs to accommodate it.

One unfortunate effect of concentrating on reasoning to means that are either sufficient or necessary is that it tempts one to think of what is going on in terms of the sort of logical shape, or form, that we find in formal deductive reasoning. If I have an end and discern a necessary means, it is very tempting to display my reasoning in a form analogous to *modus tollens* (where E is the end and M is the means), thus:

E
If not M, then not E
So: M

Now this is all very horrible, logically speaking. The E at issue here looks as if it needs to be expressible in propositional form, if the analogy with *modus tollens* is to hold. But every propositional formulation seems to be wrong. Consider the following list:

E1   I will achieve E
E2   I want (to achieve) E
E3   E is to be achieved
E4   Her illness will be cured (this being my aim)
E5   I intend to achieve E
E6   I am to achieve E

M will vary accordingly. The M in the second premise might be:

M1   I will adopt means M
M2   I will succeed in executing means M
M3   M is to be achieved—and so on.

None of this is very convincing, mainly because the M in the conclusion ought to be the taking of means M, but if it is, no such thing can appear on the left-hand side of an implication in the second premise. Worse is the fact that if we are to model reasoning to a necessary means in this way, as analogous to *modus tollens*, we will have to model reasoning to a sufficient means in the same way, this:

E
If M, then E
So: M

And on any ordinary understanding, this is a fallacy; but reasoning to a sufficient means should not be modelled on a fallacy. Such reasoning is capable of making a perfectly good case for taking the means—indeed, the case it makes seems to be even better, and better in a relevant way, than the case made by reasoning to a necessary means. After all, if I can locate a sufficient means, I know that I can achieve my end, whereas a merely necessary means may itself get me no nearer achieving my end; it may merely ward off present impediments. What is more, the case made for M—that is, for taking the means—is even stronger if the means is also sufficient than it would be if it was only necessary. The reasoning itself is the tracking of the case made, or the construction of that case, and that tracking, or constructing, does not itself get better if the means is shown to be both necessary and sufficient; it is the case constructed that becomes stronger. Of course if you don't take a necessary means to your end, you won't achieve it. But you can take any number of necessary means and be not a lot nearer achieving your end; all you may have done is to prevent it from becoming unachievable (or false, if E is understood propositionally). By contrast, if you take a sufficient means, you are there all in one swoop. So if a means is both necessary and sufficient, the case for taking that means is stronger than it would be if the means were either merely necessary or merely sufficient.

These issues about the relation between reasoning to a necessary and to a sufficient means are of course invisible to those who unwarily suppose that reasoning to a necessary means is the only form that instrumental reasoning can take.

I may take a necessary means grudgingly, as an annoying precaution, but surely that attitude would be out of place if the means turns out to be also sufficient. In our (entirely bogus) logical formulations, however, a case where a means is both necessary and sufficient would have this structure:

E
If not M, then not E
If M, then E
So: M

And adding the third premise to the second does not improve the case for M in any way at all. Whatever force the original version had (the inference to a necessary means), it cannot be added to in this way. So this 'logical' way of understanding the situation fails to capture the nature of the relevant reasoning, since it prevents us from showing how the fact that a necessary means is also sufficient strengthens the case for taking that means.

Kenny suggests that practical reasoning can be understood as theoretical reasoning upside down (1975: ch. 5). The inferences that are valid in theoretical reasoning are valid in reverse in practical reasoning. So in theoretical reasoning we have A→AvB, but in practical reasoning that would be terrible, since any reason would be a reason to do anything and everything; so what we have instead is AvB→A (I must do one or the other, so I'll do this one), which on the theoretical side would be a fallacy. Again, in theoretical reasoning one has A&B→A, while in practical reasoning one might have A→A&B (as where in order to invite her, I invite her husband too). But this runs straight up against the problem already mentioned, that if we think that the valid form of practical instrumental reasoning is reasoning to a necessary means, one renders reasoning to a sufficient means invalid, and if one thinks the valid form is reasoning to a sufficient means (which is ordinarily thought of as the fallacy of asserting the consequent) one renders reasoning to a necessary means a fallacy. But they are neither of them fallacies; they are both cogent forms of reasoning. So, as I said above, what we need to understand is how it is that reasoning to a means that is both sufficient and necessary is somehow more cogent (in the sense that the case for action is stronger) than is reasoning to a means that is sufficient but not necessary, and more cogent than is reasoning to a means that is necessary but not sufficient. Nobody seems to have shown us how to do this. And what is more, there does seem to be some difference in cogency between reasoning to a necessary means and reasoning to a sufficient one, and nobody has shown us how to think of that either.

In these remarks, the notion of cogency at issue is that of the strength of the case made for taking the means.

7.4 A Better Approach

The solution to these quandaries is to abandon the attempt to display instrumental reasoning in pseudo-logical form. Instead we shall have to think of the matter differently. In the terms I have proposed earlier, it should seem obvious that when faced with the following situation:

E is worth achieving, and if I don't do M E will become unattainable at least in some cases I see reason to do M. So, taking the symbols out so as to check on the coherence of what we are saying: her recovery is worth achieving, and if I don't get hold of the necessary tablets she will not recover—these two considerations, taken together, manifestly favour getting hold of the necessary tablets. If we were to add that if I do get hold of the tablets, she will recover, the case made for getting hold of the tablets is even stronger. We have two ways of understanding how that increase in strength occurs. We can say that the fact that the means is sufficient intensifies the reason given us by the fact that that means is necessary (or vice versa, or maybe even both), or we can say that the necessity and the sufficiency of the means are two independent reasons. We could even say both of these things. (More on this below, at the end of 9.7.)

What if we consider by itself the fact that the means is sufficient for our end? We have abandoned the attempt to display the reason given us by that fact in pseudo-logical terms, because doing so turned good reasoning into a fallacy. Do the two facts, that the end is worth achieving and that this course of action will deliver it, combine to favour taking this course of action? I would have thought it obvious that in any ordinary case they do.

Admittedly, one can imagine cases in which they might seem not to. I need some money for a worthy cause and killing my parents will secure me that money, if I can manage to get away with it. Are we to say that these considerations give me *some* reason to kill my parents off, one to be set against any reason I might have not to do that? There are various ways of avoiding that awkwardness, such as an appeal to John McDowell's conception of silencing. McDowell supposes that the prospect of carnal pleasure is a reason to commit adultery that is silenced as a reason by the wrongness of what is proposed. (This is another form of relation between reasons to be added to those I mentioned in 3.3–3.5.) Now this thought about silencing can come in two forms (Seidman 2005). The first is that the prospect of carnal pleasure ceases to be a reason at all, being silenced; the second is that it remains a reason, but a silenced one. In the first form, we avoid maintaining that I have some reason to kill my parents off. In the second, we apparently do not avoid that, but our admission that it is a reason is explicitly deprived of practical relevance. If we find this last possibility hard to make sense of, that will be because we see no way of depriving something that is still a reason from having practical relevance. A third McDowellian move, therefore, would be to say that it is deprived of practical relevance for us because we are 'seeing matters aright'. I think this has to mean that though it does favour killing them off, that favouring is one to which someone seeing matters aright would be entirely indifferent.

Finally, there will be no difficulty in capturing the force of reasoning to a partial means. The fact that driving to Birmingham will get me part of the way to Edinburgh, with a good chance of picking up further transport thereafter, makes a perfectly good case for doing that. The fact that there are other equally good methods of making progress towards my end does not undermine that case in any way.

7.5 A Difficulty

The account I have given of practical reasoning was designed initially to capture the nature of moral deliberation. The practical deliberator has, as one might put it, a merely formal aim of working out how to proceed in the situation in which she finds herself. This is rather like the formal aim we can ascribe to the theoretical reasoner, which is merely to work out what to believe given the evidence available. These ends, which I am calling formal, can be contrasted with ends to be called material, which we have when we are deliberating with a view to a material end. A moral deliberator, whose formal aim is merely to act in morally defensible ways, may be trying to work out whether she should devote some of her income to charitable purposes. Here her aim is not merely formal: it is the material one of doing the right thing with respect to philanthropy. Her question becomes more material when she tries to decide which charity is the one that her contributions will enable to do the most good. Here she has an antecedent material end, something she has already decided on, and her question now concerns which means to take to that end.

Instrumental reasoning is reasoning to a material end, in this sense. But if we are to make such reasoning consonant with the picture I have been presenting so far, we have to confront two sorts of difficulty. These difficulties both arise because it is very tempting to present the first premise of instrumental reasoning in some form such as 'my end is to V' or just 'I want to V'.

The first difficulty is that the fact that one has an end is not itself a reason to pursue that end, nor to adopt any means, nor even to adopt the most efficient means. So its role among the considerations that together favour the course of action to be taken is dubious. I take the basic point at issue to have been established by Joseph Raz (among others including Warren Quinn (1993)). Just as having a desire gives one no reason to satisfy that desire unless the thing desired is something that there is some reason to desire, so having an end that one has no reason to have gives one no reason to take steps to achieve that end, even if it makes it more probable that one will take those steps. (This is true even though having E as one's end is not just desiring E. People desire lots of things that they have not adopted as an end. Still, when they do, they are in a position to reason instrumentally to ways of satisfying those desires.) There is no room for bootstrapping here; one cannot give oneself reasons to pursue an end by adopting that end as one's own, if one had no reasons to adopt that end in the first place.

I said that this point has been established by Raz and Quinn, which is a strong claim. But even if it emerges that there are still some ways in which our desires can make a difference to the reasons we have, it looks as if instrumental reasoning recognizes no restrictions on those ways at all. *Any* aim (or perhaps any desire) is good enough to reason from, while not all aims or desires are such that merely having them generates a reason to pursue them.

Well, perhaps one cannot always give oneself reasons in this way, but by adopting an end one might be able to alter the normative score in some other way. One might suggest, for instance, that there is a rational requirement (or something weaker than a requirement, perhaps just a reason) of this form: if you have end E, do not obstruct it. (Here obstructing is acting in such a way as to militate against one's achieving that end.) If so, by adopting an end one puts oneself in the grips of this requirement. But the reply to this is that failing to take a sufficient means is not any sort of obstruction of one's end. It is only failing to take a necessary means that does that. So this appeal to rational requirements will not work across the board.

So we are left thinking that adopting an end does not itself, or always, give one a reason to pursue it. And this makes trouble for my general account of practical reasoning because, though the fact that one has a certain end is undeniably relevant in some way to the nature of one's reasoning, its relevance is not that of favouring certain courses of action. Nor, it seems, can it be said to intensify any independent reason one has to pursue that end. (Though perhaps this suggestion is worth taking more seriously.) Nor, I would say, does it enable other considerations to be reasons that they would not otherwise have been. So how are we to understand instrumental reasoning within the constraints that I have accepted, or rather imposed?

One possibility is to appeal to the idea that anyone who adopts an end sees something to be said for the pursuit of that end. So we can reasonably ascribe to that person a belief that the end is worth pursuing. And that thing believed, that the end is worth pursuing, could indeed be part of a set of considerations that together favour acting in one way rather than another. In this indirect way we might hope to capture the practical relevance of the fact that the end has been adopted.

If this suggestion—which Raz, for instance, seems to find plausible enough in his (2011: ch. 4)—could be sustained, it would make it possible for me to display the nature of instrumental reasoning without difficulty. The reasoner reasons from such a (supposed) fact as 'E would be worth achieving, if I could' and a supporting fact such as 'here is an opportunity to take at least some steps in that direction' or 'doing this would get me there all in one swoop' or 'if I don't do this, I won't be able to achieve E', to action in the service of that end.

The worry I have about relying on this suggestion (which first appeared in the previous section) is that though it works perfectly well on appropriate occasions, it may be too heavy-handed if imposed on all instances of instrumental reasoning. Just as one can find oneself desiring something that one does not see any reason to desire—we just want it, that's all—we can have an aim without seeing anything much to be said for it. Even if, when we first adopted the aim, we saw something good in it, we may just have forgotten about that, or even changed our mind without noticing it.

All these points depend, however, on writing the first premise as 'I want to V' or 'My aim is to V.' The autobiographical aspect of these formulations is what leaves them open to the worry that wanting something or making it one's aim does not itself generate any reason to act in one way rather than another. Matters would be different if we abandon these autobiographical formulations and, in the sort of way that Anscombe suggested in *Intention* (1957: §§34ff.), express the major premise using what she called a 'desirability characterization'. The idea here is that one reasons, not from such things as 'I want a cow', but from such things as that having a cow would be useful, pleasant, amusing, a return to normality, shocking to the neighbours, or just a bit of a change. In each case the major premise is presented in such a way that value is already involved or imputed, and there is no tendency to reinterpret that premise as some remark about oneself.

The difficulty about this reworking of the major premise is that it deprives us of a supposed advantage, derived from the supposed principle that one cannot get out of sound reasoning anything more than what one has put in. The idea that instrumental reasoning is reasoning from intention to intention is one expression of that idea. If the 'premises' do not contain any mention of an intention, no intention can emerge as the conclusion. Anscombe's way of representing matters simply flies in the face of this intuition. But I do not think of this as any sort of weakness, as one might expect of someone who thinks that one can reason to action from 'premises' that do not include an action (whatever that might mean).

7.6 Another Difficulty about Autobiographical Premises

There is a second type of difficulty that arises if we express the starting point of deliberation in autobiographical form. There will be a question whether the worry applies as much to aims as to desires, but I start with desires. Such autobiographical premises are very hard to make good sense of. Anthony Price (2008: ch. 1) offers us a nice pair of examples:

> I want to get drunk every night.
> If I work in a pub it will be easy to get drunk every night
> So I'll work in a pub.

And:

> I want to get drunk every night
> If I work in a pub it will be easy to get drunk every night
> So the last place I should work in is a pub.

The difference lies, of course, in the reasoner's attitude to his own desire. In the first case, he is taking the desire as a given and is reasoning towards satisfying that desire. In the second, he is taking the fact that he has that desire as a feature of the situation that needs to be accommodated. This account of the difference is not yet very perspicuous, or perspicacious; but I find some help in the distinction between a desire as a commitment and a desire as a predicament. My personal example is an advertisement I saw on a bus in Washington, DC, which asked, 'Do you always want to look at pornography? If so, call this number.' The number given was that of a clinic rather than that of a good source of pornography.

If we are to represent our starting point in this apparently autobiographical form, then, how are we to cope with the fact that reference to a desire can, as it seems, play either of these two very different roles? One way of trying to do that is to pack the premises appropriately. So we might add to Price's second reasoning the premise 'Someone who wants to get drunk every night ought not to put themselves in the way of temptation,' and hope that this would make the right sort of difference. But it won't make any difference, if the reasoner is not already treating the first premise (I want to get drunk every night) in the right (that is, the second, sensible) way. And if he is treating it in that way, this additional premise is technically redundant. If he is not, the addition of that premise is practically irrelevant; it is like the addition of an 'I know this is not a good idea but . . .'

One might also suppose that, since the issue concerns the reasoner's attitudes to his own desires, the solution is to add a second-order attitude to the disputed first-order attitude. So the sensible alcoholic might add, 'I don't want to want to get drunk every night,' and this distinguishes his position from that of the willing drinker. But this manoeuvre simply faces the same issue again at second intension. The reasoner's attitude to his second-order desire will need to be brought in, and so on ad infinitum.

This issue is relevant to all first-personal premises of this sort. We need to find a way of showing their relevance that does not amount to the insertion of further premises. It is as if the reasoner is a person with a practical problem to which he is looking for a solution of a certain sort, but that he is looking for a solution of that sort is not itself one of the matters of fact he is reasoning from. It is more like an expression of the nature of the problem he is trying to solve. So someone who reasons: 'there are cows in the Hereford market, so I'll go there' is someone who wants a cow. He does not need to add the autobiographical premise 'I want a cow' to the reasoning. He is a person whose question is 'How can I get a cow?', and this is for him a practical question rather than an idle query in an idle moment, as in 'How could I get a cow, if I wanted one?'[2]

Not only this, but he is not a person who will get himself a cow no matter what the cost (in financial or other terms). It may be that investigation of the availability of cows will cause him to give up the search, perhaps because it is too expensive or because he comes to see that it is inappropriate in some way—a goat would be altogether better. The process of reasoning to an end can cause one to abandon that end. One's question then, is not exactly 'How can I get a cow?', but rather something like 'How can I get a cow, if indeed I am to do that?' The standard philosophical example at the moment is that of reasoning to a suitable means to attending a conference. One's question then is 'How can I get to this conference, if indeed I am to do that?'; this formulation leaves it open that the considerations adduced in the reasoning may lead one to abandon the aim which informed one's reasoning in the first place. So one might think: I can charter a private plane, but that is way too expensive—and so on for all alternative forms of travel, and so give up one's plan to attend the conference. And this would be a form of practical reasoning; it is reasoning from the unsuitability of all practicable means to the abandoning of the end. But it is hard to conceive of this as reasoning from the end, or from having that end, to its abandonment.

In this section I have cast my practical reasoner as asking herself a practical question: 'How am I to go about getting a cow, if indeed I am to do that?' rather than starting from some form of 'I want'. Sebastian Rödl suggested to me an alternative device, which abandons the autobiographical premise 'I want a cow' and replaces it with a gerundive premise of the form 'a cow is to be bought'. This is a promising suggestion, which has the advantage of offering something that can itself be believed, but which carries its practical relevance on its face in a way that does not seem to depend on the presence of a desire. One could still ask whether everyone who has an aim thinks of their object as 'to be pursued'. But I think the

---

[2] For a similar point, see Price (2011: n. 70).

answer to that might be that if they don't, they are not going to be in the business of reasoning from it to ways of achieving it.

The question then becomes what is the relation between my appeal to a practical question and Rödl's appeal to a gerundive. After all, a Roman (Cato) who starts from 'delenda est Carthago' (Carthage is to be destroyed) then asks himself the question, 'How are we to do that?—if indeed we are.' I don't mean to suggest that this question needs to be explicitly raised, merely that it is in the offing as he deliberates. So it may be that the gerundive approach and the appeal to a practical question are not in the end very different. The advantage of Rödl's suggestion is that, unlike a question, it offers something from or towards which one can reason.

I don't really see either of these suggestions as more than elaborations of Anscombe's suggestion that the major premise of instrumental reasoning specifies an outcome under a 'desirability characterisation'. Adding the 'how am I to get that?' question to an outcome specified as desirable in a certain respect turns what would otherwise be a mere comment on the value of some possibility (having a cow) into the starting point of a practical enquiry.

7.7 The Relevance of the Autobiographical

The question then is to what extent this addition to the picture I have been offering is really consonant with the picture itself, rather than an ad hoc addition that has been forced on me by what I take to be the correct view that (generally, at least) wanting to do something gives one no reason to do what one wants, even if one has some (other) reason to want it, and that having an end gives one no reason to take means to that end unless there is reason to adopt the end in the first place.

In my defence, it is worth pointing out that all theories have to deal with the point that we owe to Anscombe, and originally to Anselm Müller,[3] that merely adding a premise about desire does not yet tell us how the reasoner is treating that desire, and that the best way to do that is to take the reference to the desire out of the premises altogether. So this point, at least, cannot be suspected of suspect motivation.

---

[3] Anscombe says in her (1974: §2) that 'I owe the point and example to A. Müller.'

Some think, by contrast, that there must at least be a formal reference to desire among the premises—even as the major premise—because practical reasoning is motivational, and only something that appeals to a desire that the agent already has can be motivational in the way required: see for example Audi (2006: 4.4). This would explain, for instance, why reference to someone else's desire will not serve the desired purpose. Even if his wanting me to stop is recognized by me as a reason, it is not going to be one that can generate a motivation to desist unless there is some desire of mine to which it can be related, for example a desire not to get into his bad books. If this point is good, it is good whether one identifies a desire with a motivatedness, or whether one thinks of the desire as that which motivates.

I take this to be a mistaken way of thinking. As I see it, desire and motivation arise in response to the prospect of some (supposed) good or evil. We explain that motivatedness by pointing out the good supposedly to be achieved or the evil to be avoided. We are not reduced to explaining motivation only as derived from some antecedent motivation, so that it is either brute and unexplained, or else derived. Motivation can be both brute and explained; we explain it by showing that the thing desired is of a sort that it is perfectly sensible to desire.

So I don't see any need for all practical reasoning to start from a desire that is already somehow given, the only question being whether or how one is to implement it. But practical reasoning does not occur in the void either. It is enquiry, but not idle enquiry; it is enquiry that serves a practical purpose. To have a practical purpose is to want something, or to have an aim. But when I reason in the service of an aim, I do not need to reason from having that aim. I reason to ways of achieving what I want, of realizing some aim that I have, but my reasoning need not start autobiographically, from the fact that I want this or have that aim.

First, all practical reasoning is beset by constraints of various sorts. A proposed course of action can be rejected as too expensive, as too uncaring, as dull, as conflicting with other equally serious concerns—or for many other reasons. So it is a constraint on one's reasoning that it take us to action that does not conflict with (too many) other purposes that we may have, even though there is no need to specify which purposes and how significant a conflict in advance. Second, not all practical reasoning is conducted in response to the formal question 'What am I to do here?' Our question is often material. This is what gives colour to the thought that practical reasoning is the process of searching for, and evaluating, ways of implementing an existing purpose, desire, or aim. But that one starts with a purpose, or with several purposes, does not mean that one is reasoning from having it, or them. And one cannot reason from a purpose itself. But one can reason to a purpose (*contra* Hume).

7.8 Extending the Anscombe–Müller Point

How are we to capture the idea that not every consideration adduced in deliberation is presented either as a reason or as an enabler, or in any other of the forms we originally distinguished? I have in mind such things as the aim, if the agent has an aim, or the generally unvoiced constraints within which deliberation takes place, which when violated lead to a kind of abortion of the reasoning. I said above that we could think of the agent as starting from a practical question posed by an aim that she has, such as 'How am I to get a cow?' Then I expanded that so as to leave room for the relevance of the unvoiced constraints, so that it came to be 'How am I to get a cow, if indeed I am to do that?' But if one does treat things this way, it appears that the answer to that question will have to be an action. Does that make enough sense?

One interesting question is whether the Anscombe–Müller point applies as much to belief, to intention, and to having an aim as it does to desire. There is a reason for thinking that it does not, which is that one can treat one's desire as an odd fact about oneself without ceasing to have the desire and even without in some way diminishing the force of one's identification with it. But if I try to run the same idea with belief, I hit considerations to do with Moore's paradox. Someone who says to himself 'I believe that p: I wonder if I am right to do so' is already to some extent standing back from his commitment to its being the case that p. If one wonders if one is right, that is, if it is the case that p, as one supposes, one is no longer really supposing that p. The sense of one's wonderment is rather 'I wonder if it is the case that p, as I have been supposing.'

Now ask the same question about aims: can someone say 'my aim is to achieve end E, but I am beginning to wonder whether that is really a sensible aim'? Here again it seems that just in asking the question, he has put his aim into abeyance, into quarantine as it were. It is as if he had asked, 'up to now my aim has been to achieve end E, but I am beginning to wonder whether that was really a sensible aim'.

If this point is good, it should apply to intentions as well. This would mean that the Anscombe–Müller point does not apply to aims, to intentions, and to beliefs in quite the same way that it does to desires. For one can question one's desires without ceasing to desire or standing back in some way from that desire; one's question is more whether to fight that motivation. The question then is what significance this might have for the account we give of instrumental reasoning.

And the answer is that it does not make much difference and we can all relax.

There were two sorts of reason why 'I want to V' cannot properly be represented as a premise in reasoning, or as a consideration that contributes to one's deliberations in the same sort of way as other matters of fact (real or supposed). The first was Raz's point, that aims and desires that one has no reason to have give one no new reason to pursue or implement them. The second was the Anscombe–Müller point that there is more than one way to take autobiographical premises of this sort. We have decided that the latter point applies less to intentions, aims, and beliefs than it does to desires. But even if that decision can be defended, there remains Raz's point to be dealt with, and that point applies to beliefs and intentions as much as to aims and desires. A belief that one has no reason to have gives one no reason to believe its consequences. And an intention that one has no reason to have, or to form, gives one no reason to implement it. Still, we responded to the Raz point by supposing that reference to aims and intentions can be located within the practical question that the deliberator is addressing without any suggestion that having an aim gives one a reason to pursue it, and the same manoeuvre will apply to desires. With beliefs, the situation may be slightly different, but nobody ever supposed (I hope) that a belief that one has without any reason nevertheless gives one some reason to believe its consequences. So premises of the form 'I believe that p' are harmless, and operate as does any other premise; that I believe that p is a circumstance that may favour certain courses of action in just the same sort of way as that she believes that p. That I believe I am essentially superior to my fellows is a very good reason for me to think again, and for them to take me down a peg or two.

7.9 Doubting and Hoping

Thinking about these autobiographical premises and the role that they play in reasoning leads one to consider the role of apparently similar premises about doubt and hope. Suppose that someone, call him Hesitator, doubts that p, realizes that if q then p, and so comes to doubt whether q. Encouraged by the (perhaps specious) clarity of our grids, we might try to map the progress of Hesitator's thought, his reasoning, thus:

Doubt	p
Belief	If q then p
Doubt	q

There could be another person, Dehesitator, who doubts whether p, realizes that if q then p, and so ceases to doubt whether p. The grid for Dehesitator might be:

Doubt	p
Belief	If q then p
Belief	p

But what is going on here really is that Dehesitator is willing to accept q independently, and we failed to cater for that in our grid. Dehesitator's thought is not 'if q then p', but 'since q, p'. The grid should be:

Doubt	p
Belief	If q then p
Belief	q
Belief	p

Here there is no issue, because the actual reasoning is straightforward, even if Dehesitator started off doubting whether p rather than simply neither believing nor disbelieving it. The reasoning proper, as I would say, begins on the second line. So let us return to Hesitator.

Unfortunately, the way we have represented Hesitator's train of thought is definitely wrong. We represented him as reasoning from something that he doubts, and this is impossible. To reason from something, one has to accept it, or at least to act as if one accepts it. (I added this extra possibility in order to avoid ruling out reasoning from supposition. But that is quite distinct from reasoning from something that one doubts.) We can see our mistake when we add the mapping to the grid, thus:

Doubt	*p*
Belief *favour*	if *q* then *p*
Doubt	*q*

One thing that Hesitator accepts is that he doubts whether *p*. This might mislead us into proposing the following grid:

Belief	I doubt that *p*
Belief	If *q* then *p*
Doubt	*q*

What is wrong with this is that it is not the (supposed) facts that if *q* then *p* and that he doubts that *p* that favour his doubting that *q*. (Though such facts might have something to say about the rationality of his position, or process.)

If we want something that definitely does favour doubting that *q*, we might try this:

Belief	It is doubtful whether *p*
Belief	If *q* then *p*
Doubt	*q*

Here we have two things that Hesitator might be willing to sign up to, and they combine to favour doubting whether q. Call this grid GD. Of course one might move in the opposite direction, à la Dehesitator:

Belief	It is doubtful whether p
Belief	If q then p
Belief	q
Belief	p

But, as before, this is really equivalent, as reasoning, to

Belief	If q then p
Belief	q
Belief	p

The doubting was just a state that Dehesitator was in before he started reasoning. It is not as if one starts all reasoning to the belief that q with the statement 'I do not yet believe that q'. This would not be helpful.

Let us return to GD above. What is unsatisfactory with this grid, quite apart from the fact that it converts all doubt into a belief about dubiousness, is that we would need to play a similar trick with hope, and this is harder. A grid for hopeful reasoning might look like this:

Hope	p
Belief	If q then p
Hope	q

I hope that my daughter has got home safely; the grid reveals the form in which we are rendering the apparently autobiographical premise 'I hope that p.' Believing that she would have done so if she had managed to catch the train, I hope that she caught the train. This looks like a train of reasoning—and of course it could be considerably more complicated than this. But can one reason from something that one merely hopes to be true? I think not. We could try converting hoping that p into an appropriate belief, on these lines:

Belief	It is to be hoped that p
Belief	If q then p
Hope	q

And indeed hoping that q is something that could be favoured by the two considerations in the right-hand column above. A more complex version might be:

Belief	It is to be hoped that p
Belief	If q then p
Belief	It is to be hoped that q
Hope	q

But the hope that q is really favoured by this consideration alone, that it is to be hoped that q. The reasoning, if there is any here at all, stops with the third belief.

Admittedly, someone who believes that it is to be hoped that p need not actually hope that p. But this is not a difficulty, because the grid does not suggest otherwise. As far as the grid is concerned, what is required runs the other way: that any person who hopes that p believes that it is to be hoped that p—so that our grid can start with a belief rather than with a hope. Unfortunately I find it hard to persuade myself that one can legislate in this way. So at the moment I don't see how to capture reasonings of this sort. The only thing I can say in self-defence is that the problems here are not problems just for me. I have never seen these issues discussed, and the difficulties they raised will presumably infect any theory of reasoning that allows reasoning from hope and from doubt.

8

Reasoning to Normative Belief

In this chapter I consider the first of two views that are opposed to mine. This, the more trenchant, is Joseph Raz's claim that the only thing worth calling practical reasoning is reasoning to what one might call 'practical beliefs'.

8.1 Three Views

As I said at the beginning of Chapter 1 (1.2), there are three views about the sort of reasoning that is worth calling practical. They differ in their account of the output, or 'conclusion'. Raz holds that such reasoning can only lead to the formation of what one might call a practical belief: that is, to such a belief as that there is most reason to V, or that one ought to V, or that V-ing is the thing to do, or that there is good reason to do this and no more reason to do anything else. (This list can be left open-ended.) Against Raz, John Broome holds that reasoning is not restricted to the formation of belief. Practical reasoning is reasoning whose output is the formation of an intention. By 'intention' here he means a plan of action, or a plan to act; and a plan to act is distinct from the action planned. My view, however, is that though one can reason to a practical belief, and one can reason to the formation of intention, one can also reason to the (or an) action commended, recommended, or called for by the situation as the reasoning has shaped it up.

To repeat: the neo-Aristotelian view is that reasoning to action is just as direct and unmediated as is reasoning to belief and to intention. The considerations we adduce in deliberation can lead us to act, or to form an intention to act, without passing through a most-reasons belief or anything else of that sort. And an action done in response to considerations adduced will be intentional in a way that does not mean that it is necessarily the product of a prior intention. All this is compatible with the Primacy of the Practical, for that thesis generated an asymmetry of explanation rather than a temporal order of some sort. It does not follow from the Primacy of the Practical that reasoning to belief and to intention is somehow indirect.

My attitudes to the views of Raz and of Broome differ, however. Nobody denies that there is reasoning to moral judgement or to practical belief more generally, and I have no particular quarrel with Raz's account of what is involved in this process. The only question between Raz and me is whether there is an analogous process of reasoning to action. With Broome the matter is different. I agree that there is reasoning to the formation or adjustment or abandoning of intention, but I don't accept Broome's picture of how this works.

The structure of the debate at this point is quite interesting. To the extent that Broome's view can be defended against Raz, it may be that my more distant view can acquire a similar immunity. And if Broome's view turns out to be vulnerable to some of Raz's arguments, it may yet be that my more extreme view can defend itself against them. So let us see how it goes, starting with Raz.

In his first attempt at this topic (1978: Introduction, pp. 5–6), Raz saw the battleground roughly as I have just outlined it, with three possibilities on offer and fighting it out between them. In his next attempt (2011), he hardly mentions the neo-Aristotelian view and devotes his attention mainly to demolishing Broome's view. And there is more recently (2015) a third attempt, which pays far more attention to the Aristotelian approach.

That Raz has had three goes at this topic makes treatment of his contributions difficult, because arguments he relied on earlier seem to vanish in later papers, leaving one wondering whether he has abandoned them or not. So in what follows, I may be partly responding to arguments that Raz would no longer make.

8.2 Raz's First Argument: Failure to Act and Rational Fault

Raz's first argument starts from the fact that you can fail to act in the way most favoured by your reasoning without being rationally at fault. If they hold you down and prevent you from doing the relevant action, the fact that you have not managed to act in the way most favoured by the considerations adduced in your reasoning in no way impugns either your reasoning or your rationality. But it ought to, if the reasoning *includes* the action most favoured—as it would if the action were the conclusion of that reasoning. The reasoning would be incomplete; you would have failed to draw the conclusion you ought to have drawn, and you would be criticizable for that. But you are not criticizable at all. So the action cannot be part of the reasoning.

My reply to this is that the reasoning is indeed incomplete, since one is failing to respond in the way most favoured by the considerations adduced. In failing to respond in that way, one is failing to act as one has most reason to act. But this does not establish that there is any rational failure, since there is no rational requirement that one complete one's reasoning.

Let us consider the matter from another angle, and ask whether Raz's point, if good, is also good against Broome's view that reasoning can take one to forming an intention but never to acting. Is it the case that you might be prevented (by other people, or even by the demands of the situation) from forming the relevant intention? If so, your failure so to intend would in no way impugn your rationality or your reasoning, since rationality did not require you not to be prevented in this way. A little imagination might help here. Suppose, when you get to that stage in your reasoning, you have seen where it is taking you but have not yet committed yourself to the relevant course of action by forming the intention so to act. Suddenly the door opens and in rush your three grandchildren, all ready for an afternoon at the zoo—at which point you forget about the whole thing and never return to it, since once you get back from the zoo it is too late. Now: how do you stand from the rational point of view (if there is such a thing, analogous to the famous moral point of view)? Is it that, rationally speaking, you ought to have committed yourself by forming the relevant intention? Somehow I doubt it. Is it that your reasoning is incomplete? Yes, I would say, but that incompleteness is not something for which you are (in this case) at fault.

Of course in other cases you might be at fault, but this is not enough to establish that the fault at issue is a failure of rationality.

Turn now to a case of belief-formation. You are wondering what is the correct answer to a complex financial question. Considering all the relevant issues, you can see where they are taking you but it is tricky and you have not yet committed yourself on the point. Then the grandchildren arrive, etc. . . . Now: is it that rationality requires that you commit yourself to a certain answer to your question, so that rationally speaking you ought to accept it as the answer? I doubt it. Is it that your reasoning is incomplete? Yes, I would say, but that incompleteness is not something for which you are at fault.

So why should we not say the same about practical reasoning? You can have done the deliberating, seen where it is going, but not yet committed yourself. (The act of will has not yet been performed, if you like.) First, in this case too we can say that you have not failed to do what rationality requires of you. Second, you are in just the same situation with respect to the response called for by your practical reasoning as you were with respect to the response called for by your planning reasoning (an awkward name, I know) and with respect to the cognitive response called for by your theoretical reasoning. So in this case too your reasoning is incomplete. None of this does anything to show that action cannot stand to the considerations adduced in reasoning in exactly the same direct relation that belief can stand.

Raz does have a further view about the relevant difference between reasoning to action and reasoning to belief. He writes:

One who believes that there is a conclusive case for the truth of a proposition cannot but believe that proposition (pathological cases aside). There is no gap, no extra step, between believing that the case for the proposition is conclusive and believing the proposition.   (2011: 38)

This is why reasoning to action is always relevantly different; in reasoning to action there is not this way of closing the gap, because there is no such thing as a conclusive case for action (though one might ask why not). But even if Raz were right about this, it would not be sufficient to sustain his general position. For what of the much more common cases where the case for believing the conclusion is good enough, but not conclusive? Would Raz have to allow that in such cases there is always an intermediate stage? Would he really want to say that one cannot reason directly to any belief at all, except when the reasoning generates a conclusive case? This appeal to the conclusive case is a two-edged sword.[1]

---

[1] There is a good discussion of this issue in Fernandez (2016).

8.3 Acting for Simple, and for Complex, Reasons

I expect a certain response to some of these suggestions, which is that they give the game away with their talk of 'seeing where the reasoning is going', and the contrast between that and the relevant commitment. This can really be nothing more than a belief, or perhaps just a hunch, that this course of action is the one most favoured by the considerations adduced, taken as whole. And once one allows that, Raz's position is vindicated.

But what are we to say about analogous cases in which we are dealing, not with deliberation, but with simple acting for a reason? We don't want to say that nobody is capable of acting for a reason except by way of a belief to the effect that there is a reason here. First, this threatens to lead to an infinite regress of reason-beliefs, in the following way. If I cannot act for a reason without believing that there is such a reason to act, surely I cannot believe for a reason without believing that there is such a reason to believe. And this will generate a regress until we hit a belief that there is a reason which is held for no reason at all.

Second, the requirement that there be a reasons-belief wherever one responds to a reason seems to over-intellectualize something that does not need to be so sophisticated. So when one acts for a reason, we will want to say that one was sensitive to the presence of that reason, without meaning to commit ourselves to the view that this sensitivity necessarily amounts to a belief that the reason is there.

If an action can in this way be a direct response to a reason, mediated by the relevant sensitivity, why cannot an action be a direct response to a more complex conception of the situation, arrived at by deliberation? The complexity of the conception, or of the situation as conceived, seems perfectly compatible with the directness of the response. That one has to think harder, or longer, does not show that the only possible direct response is something other than action. Nor does it show that a sensitivity to the tendency of the deliberation is to be conceived as a belief about its conclusion.

If we do allow that someone can see where the reasoning is going without yet making the relevant commitment, those who, with Raz, hold that this commitment is not part of the reasoning will have to say the same of belief, and will thus be committed to saying that believing that p is never the conclusion of theoretical reasoning, since it is never a proper part of that reasoning. If, by contrast, we are willing to say that the concluding that *p* is itself part of the reasoning, we should say the same of the action most favoured by the considerations adduced. It is all or nothing.

This debate between me and Raz is run in terms of a conception of belief as occurrent, or conscious. Our question is whether there needs to be a certain episode between the adducing of various considerations and the action done in their light. Raz thinks there needs to be such an episode and I do not. How would this debate be run if we thought in terms of belief as a functional state rather than as an episode? I could hardly deny that the agent who responds directly to the considerations favouring acting in this way is in such a functional state. He is a person disposed to act in this way when certain concerns of his are triggered.

But I would view this as victory rather than defeat. Such a person is reasoning directly from the considerations adduced to the action that those considerations favour. The belief that these considerations most favour the response (or some other such belief) is not to be understood as an intermediate stage.

8.4 Raz's More Recent Argument, against the Simple Account

Raz's most recent attempt to see off an Aristotelian view, which he calls the Simple Account, is his (2015). The core of the Simple Account is this:

Successful reasoning is recognizing that something is a reason, and responding to it, in the way it makes appropriate.

This holds any case of acting for a reason, or of responding to a reason, to be an instance of reasoning. And this is not my picture at all. What my account does is to distinguish simple acting for a reason, or acting for a simple reason, from acting in the light of various considerations that go together to make a case for acting in that way. The difference lies mainly in the complexity of the case for acting that is revealed in the process of reasoning.

Consider then this objection from Raz to the Simple Account:

But, if F is a reason for the agent to R, not all ways of coming to R when taking F to be a reason for it are cases of reasoning. For example, if I believe that John gave me a present for my last birthday because I remember his doing so, no reasoning need be involved in forming the belief, even though that I remember him doing so is a reason to believe that he did. If sound this point refutes the simple account. It does not provide a sufficient condition of reasoning to a belief any more than of reasoning to an intention [or of reasoning to an action—JD].

Believing that something happened because I remember it is not an example of the sort of process that I think of as reasoning; it is too simple. So this objection does not touch my position.

But Raz has other things to say that may have more bite. He first takes a case where someone has reasoned to a normative belief of the relevant sort (that he ought to act, has good reason to act, etc.) but does not do the action. He then asks whether the agent's reasoning was incomplete. The idea is that the reasoning is not somehow completed by the action, and so we cannot conceive of the action as the conclusion of the reasoning. But of course the reasoning in this case was not incomplete; it took him to a normative belief.

This establishes nothing. The question should be: if, having considered the relevant considerations with a view to action, I don't draw the normative conclusion-belief and I don't do the action either, has my reasoning been concluded? And the answer is no. Has it been interrupted? Probably. But nothing follows from this either.

One explanation of this failure to connect emerges a little later. This is that Raz takes it that the Simple Account is trying to offer a sufficient condition for reasoning. And there is an interesting question whether Raz's complaint that the Simple Account does not provide a sufficient condition of reasoning to a belief (or to an intention or to an action) is even relevant to my account of reasoning. Was my account ever trying to do that? I ask because of the focalist nature of my approach, discussed in Chapter 6.5. My official procedure has been to offer a few instances of practical reasoning, cases in which the agent builds a practical shape of the situation confronting her and acts accordingly, that is, in the way most favoured by the considerations adduced, taken as a whole, and then to say that anything that sufficiently resembles such a process in relevant respects is also one of reasoning. In a sense, then, I do offer a sufficient condition, but it is built on notions of 'sufficient resemblance' and 'relevant respects' that hardly lend themselves to ordinary approaches in terms of necessary and sufficient conditions.

In considering Raz's argument, it is important to remember what is at issue. My view allows that there is reasoning to such normative beliefs as that this is what I ought to do, what I have most or conclusive reason to do, what I have good enough reason to do, and so on. It merely maintains that in addition to such reasoning to beliefs, there can be reasoning directly to action, which does not pass through a normative conclusion-belief. Indeed, the relevant action can stand in just the same relation to the considerations adduced as do such normative beliefs.

The notion of directness here is not psychological. I am not just saying that no normative conclusion need occur to the mind of a practical reasoner, who can jump straight from the relevant considerations to action without passing through an intermediate belief-stage. I am saying that, yes, but only because I think that it is not merely enthymematic to pass directly from relevant considerations to action.

Nor do I think it awkward to allow that the relevant considerations favour equally directly believing that one should V, intending to V, and actually V-ing. One does not need to pass through any of these to get to either of the others. The only asymmetry is given by the Primacy of the Practical. Those considerations favour believing that one should V, and favour intending to V, *because* they favour actually V-ing. The boot is on the other—or should I say the third—foot. But this asymmetry of explanation does not generate any suggestion that only the favouring of action is direct.

8.5 Equipollence

A consideration that has often influenced Raz in the past, but does not appear in his most recent treatment of these issues, is the relevance of equipollence. Equipollence (literally, equal strength) occurs in deliberation when the case for one course of action emerges as no better or worse than the case for another. Nobody denies that this happens. And the same thing can happen when we are wondering what to believe. The difference between these cases lies in the fact that, on the practical side, the deliberator has a perfect right to select either course of action as the one to pursue. On the theoretical side, by contrast, someone who recognizes that there are two equally probable options is rationally required to abstain from judgement.

This difference between permissible responses to equipollence on the two sides is well recognized. But it is not our present concern. The concern pressed by Raz in the past, though not in his two most recent attempts at this topic, is that in cases of equipollence reasoning has done its job and has left one with a choice—and the reasoning is completely silent on which way to go, which choice to make. So the action on which one eventually decides cannot itself be part of the reasoning. Why then should it be any different in cases where the reasoning does identify a specific way of acting as that most favoured by the relevant considerations?

My answer to this question is that we should not allow our account of what one might call the bad case, when the reasoning leaves us still with a choice, to infect our account of what one might call the good case, where the reasoning does hit on one way of acting as the sort of response most favoured by the situation, taken as a whole. In the good case, acting in that way is the response most favoured by the situation, and our action is done in that light. The fact that this arrangement is sometimes subverted by the discovery of a second way of acting no less favoured than the first is irrelevant to our account of cases where this is not what is happening.

This insistence that we should not allow our account of the bad case to infect our account of the good one is the general form of a now familiar response to the argument from illusion—or to arguments from illusion in general. (See my 1995, for instance.) The terminology of good and bad cases that I used in the previous paragraph, which might otherwise seem merely prejudicial, comes directly from that discussion. And it may be that Raz has ceased to press this second argument because he has recognized the possibility of that response.

But Michael Bratman suggested to me a possible extension of the argument from equipollence.[2] According to this extension, *every* practical case is a case of equipollence; every practical case is a case where there is more than one equally good option, more than one way of acting most favoured by the reasoning. This is because reasoning can never recommend a particular action but only acting in a certain way. (This is the point that I attributed to Harold Prichard in 2.3 above.) But if that point is good, there will always be more than one action equally recommended by the reasoning, and so our admission that in cases of equipollence reasoning

---

[2] The point was made later in print by Sarah Paul (2013).

cannot take us to this action rather than to that one is going to be much more damaging than we had hoped. All cases are cases of equipollence; all cases are bad cases.

Luckily, this manoeuvre can be rejected. The Prichard point is that reasoning can at best establish a sort of blueprint for action. A blueprint for a house is a partial specification of the house to be built. No blueprint could ever be a complete specification of a house, and no blueprint aspires to achieve that impossibility. The same applies to blueprints for action. Now in genuine cases of equipollence, what the reasoning serves up is (at least) two blueprints. Each of those blueprints remains to be fleshed out, and further reasoning will do this for us, until we come to a point where we determine in action all those matters that the blueprint we decide on left undetermined (of which there will always be many). Even if we had only one blueprint, and so do *not* have equipollence proper, we would still have to flesh it out—which we would do by further reasoning, always recognizing that such reasoning will always leave many matters underdetermined; again, we determine them in action. But none of this does anything to unsettle the view that the action we light on is our direct response to the considerations adduced in reasoning.

This reply may seem to fail to appreciate the difficulty. How can a course of action be a direct response to considerations adduced, if those considerations do not select that course uniquely, but only take us to doing some action or other of the relevant type? The directness of the supposed relation between considerations and action is at odds with the fact that reasoning cannot take us to any 'particular' action at all. It gets stuck at the point when all we have is a general description; and from that point on what we eventually come to do cannot be understood as part of a process of reasoning.

There is a question, however, whether reasoning to belief is in a better situation. We should not forget that a belief is a response, and as such has many characteristics that are not determined by the reasoning that leads to it. The belief is not, as it were, particularized by its content. A belief is formed at a certain time, and that time is not mentioned in the reasoning; even if one's reasoning is impeccable, there is no time at which that reasoning requires one to start believing. Again, a belief may be reluctant or grateful, enthusiastic or grudging. These domains of variability are not as extensive as those of action in the service of reasoning, but they are there. And if they are there, the difficulty that supposedly undermines the Aristotelian account of practical reasoning should be sufficient to undermine all reasoning whatever.

More generally, however, the real point is that the idea that the action we do is not uniquely selected by the considerations we adduce is not at odds with the directness of the relation between those considerations and the action we take in their light.

8.6 Raz's Third Argument: The 'That's it' Clause

Raz claims that practical reasoning requires a 'that's it' clause; theoretical reasoning does not:

even in the absence of conflicting reasons the premises of Aristotelian practical syllogism do not warrant any conclusion, for they do not include a closure premise, like 'all other things are equal', without which no conclusion is warranted, but with which the inference is no longer distinct, being similar to probabilistic reasoning.   (2011: 131)

The problem that is supposed to be addressed by use of a 'that's it' clause is that all practical reasoning is reasoning from a limited selection of facts, those that the agent is aware of and takes to be relevant to her decision. But a deliberator knows perfectly well that there may be further facts that she is not aware of and whose relevance she is not in a position to determine. So her conclusion cannot be (in verbalized form) 'So, given all the facts, this is how I should act'; it can only be something like 'On this information, this is how I should act.' The 'that's it' clause captures this limitation. It is a closure premise.

The premise Raz mentions, 'all other things are equal', is different in the way it functions. Someone who reasons from limited information *hopes* that all other things are equal, but is in no position to assert as much. Nor does one need to be in a position to assert that all other things are equal in order to be 'warranted' in drawing one's conclusion. (Note that 'warrant' here is a technical term.) And if one did assert it, one would almost certainly be asserting something false. The real point is that in deliberation one is reasoning from what one knows to be a limited set of facts, and to be justified (or warranted) in moving from those facts to a conclusion, practical or theoretical, one must have some defence against the charge that one should have made further investigation. But such a defence can be provided by showing that, given limitations of time (or money), one was now forced to decide. This fact would, however, not need to be among the premises.

So is it true that without a closure premise, no conclusion is warranted? Myself, I doubt it. Suppose it is true. Still, one might ask why Raz supposes that this undermines any distinction between practical reasoning and probabilistic reasoning. It is true that practical reasoning would be similar in this respect; but this does nothing to show that it is not distinct from probabilistic reasoning.

Raz returns to this matter a few pages later, where he is arguing against Broome's view that one can reason to an intention (which I called 'planning reasoning' above). There Raz writes:

> One possible response is that sometimes we reason directly to the intention, without pausing to draw the conclusion that the act is one we have conclusive reason to perform. . . . The suggestion seems attractive, provided there is a form of valid reasoning that leads to an intention to F via a reasoning route that does not include as an intermediate conclusion that one must F (or has a conclusive reason to F). If such an intermediate conclusion is required then we are back where we were before. But, I will argue, there is no such valid reasoning form. First, the premises of a reasoning that would yield an intention to F as its conclusion would also entail, or at any rate warrant, the conclusion that one must F. Second, unless one reasons to the conclusion that one must F one would not be justified in forming an intention to F as a result of the reasoning. That is, though the intention may be justified it cannot be regarded as a valid result of the reasoning. The existence of reasons to F is not sufficient to justify an intention to F. The intention is justified only if the reasons are not defeated. So if the intention is the conclusion of reasoning then the reasoning must include, as an intermediate conclusion, either that the reasons to F are not defeated by the conflicting reasons, or, that the reasons to F are conclusive. But if the intermediate step is permissive, that is, merely that the reasons to F are undefeated, then the intention is not warranted by the reasoning, as has been explained before. So, if the intention is warranted by the reasoning the intermediate step must be that the reasons to F are conclusive.   (2011: 135)

This is a very complicated argument and very difficult to assess. By far the simplest way to undermine it is to show that one can run the whole argument through for reasoning to belief, thus:

> One possible response is that sometimes we reason directly to the [belief], without pausing to draw the conclusion that the belief is one we have conclusive reason to accept. . . . The suggestion seems attractive, provided there is a form of valid reasoning that leads to a belief that *p* via a reasoning route that does not

include as an intermediate conclusion that one must believe that p (or has a conclusive reason to believe that p). If such an intermediate conclusion is required then we are back where we were before. But, I will argue, there is no such valid reasoning form. First, the premises of a reasoning that would yield a belief that p as its conclusion would also entail, or at any rate warrant, the conclusion that one must believe that p. Second, unless one reasons to the conclusion that one must believe that p one would not be justified in forming a belief that p as a result of the reasoning. That is, though the belief may be justified it cannot be regarded as a valid result of the reasoning. The existence of reasons to believe that p is not sufficient to justify believing that p. The belief is justified only if the reasons are not defeated. So if the belief that p is the conclusion of reasoning then the reasoning must include, as an intermediate conclusion, either that the reasons to believe that p are not defeated by the conflicting reasons, or, that the reasons to believe that p are conclusive. But if the intermediate step is permissive, that is, merely that the reasons to believe that p are undefeated, then the belief is not warranted by the reasoning, as has been explained before. So, if the belief that p is warranted by the reasoning the intermediate step must be that the reasons to believe that p are conclusive.

So I think that what emerges here is something we have seen before, that Raz's attempts to undermine opposing accounts also undermine the one thing we all agree on, which is that there is reasoning to ought-judgements, or to beliefs about what one has most reason to do. I view this both as a *reductio ad absurdum* and as a regress. It is absurd to think that one must draw the explicit most-reasons belief in order to be justified in drawing the belief which those reasons support. And there is a regress, because one cannot be justified in believing that one's reasons for believing that p are conclusive unless one's reasons justify one in believing that one's reasons for believing that p are conclusive. But then one is required, for justification of the ground level belief that p, to believe that one has conclusive reasons to believe that one has conclusive reasons to believe that p.

The only way to avoid the awkwardness of this result is to announce, most implausibly, that there is no distinction between the meta-belief and the meta-meta-belief.

8.7 First-Person and Third-Person Reasoning

One potential difference between reasoning to a most-reasons judgement (or other such normative beliefs) and reasoning to an intention or to an action is that the most-reasons judgement can concern someone other than oneself. I cannot reason to an intention or an action of yours unless

I am in a position to decide for you what you are going to do. And the explanation of this difference, it may be said, is that the will is involved when it comes to intending or to acting, but it is not involved in the formation of opinion or judgement. (I can decide for you when your will is subordinate to my will.)

It is, however, possible to look at the matter differently. I cannot reason to a belief of yours, even if I can reason to a belief of mine about how you ought to behave. Viewed in this way, theoretical reasoning is as first-personal as are planning reasoning and practical reasoning. That my belief can concern how you should act is nothing to the point.

Perhaps the explanation of this is that in each case I can be said to form a commitment, theoretical or practical.

8.8 Counter-Attack

Raz's account has it that though we can in a sense reason to an action, this always involves reasoning to a belief and acting in the light of what we have come to believe. (And the reasoning proper is finished once the relevant belief is formed.) The alternative view is that the same considerations can take us both to a belief about what we have most reason to do and to acting in that way, and that either 'conclusion' is possible without the other.

Raz's view over-intellectualizes the situation in just the same way as would a requirement that one cannot V for the reason that p without believing that p to be a reason to V. It requires of the reasoner the explicit wielding of normative conceptions in a way that seems to render the whole transaction very heavy-handed. Now of course reasoning requires normative sensitivity. One needs to be able to distinguish what is a reason from what is not, and to respond accordingly. And perhaps only those who have the concept of a reason are capable of doing that. But this does nothing to show that the concept of a reason must be playing one role rather than another in a sound passage of reasoning.

Quite apart from this over-intellectualization, there is also the worry about focus. We distort the focus of our reasons if we suppose that they are primarily reasons for a 'most-reasons' belief, and only secondarily reasons for the intention or action itself. If anything it is the other way round—the Primacy of the Practical again.

8.9 Is Belief Action?

There is a view that in belief we are passive. In action we are active (of course!), and the formation of intention—planning in advance, or deciding now to act later—is an exercise of agency too. But beliefs just happen to us. We can put ourselves into a position in which we are likely to believe this rather than that, and do so intentionally, but the actual believing is not an exercise of the will.

Another way of drawing the same distinction is to say that we can decide to act, and decide on a plan, but we are not in a position to decide that something is so; this is the province of nature, not of the rational mind.

One argument for this view, often adduced, is that we cannot believe at will. But this is irrelevant. There are many things we can do but not do at will.

I should say that Raz has always been of the opinion that in believing we are as active as we ever are, and in this I take him to be on the side of the angels. It is not because of this (indeed, one might say that it is despite this) that he holds that practical reasoning can be no more than the formation of a practical belief. Many others are of the contrary opinion, that in believing we are passive. But I agree with Raz here. It seems to me that I can decide that something is the case, make up my mind that things are so, and adopt a view of the matter. In reasoning I am as active as I ever am. I adduce considerations, I assess their relevance, and I come to a view, or form the opinion, that things are this way rather than that. In all this I am in charge, building an ever more detailed picture of the world I live in.

9

Reasoning to Intention

This penultimate chapter is a response to John Broome's argument that all practical reasoning is reasoning to an intention, and to his account of the main forms of correct practical reasoning. He allows three such forms: that in which one comes to intend a means that one believes to be necessary for one's end (in Broome's terms, 'implied by'—see below), that in which one comes to intend a means that one thinks as good as any other for the achievement of one's end, and that in which one comes to intend an action that one believes one ought to do. I will leave the third of these aside, but argue that there are many other forms of practical reasoning that are perfectly sound, or good, or sensible, even if they do not have the special property that Broome calls 'correctness'. I will also be rejecting Broome's argument that one can only reason to intention and never to action.

I am responding to Broome's account in considerable detail, not just because it is by far the most careful and detailed available, but also because of its implication that nothing less than this can count as practical reasoning. We agree that there is reasoning to intention, but we disagree both about how this works and about whether all practical reasoning is reasoning to intention of his special sort. So I will be arguing at some length that his account is wrong even in its own terms, quite apart from issuing bizarre and under-motivated restrictions on what reasoning can be or do. And the purpose of all this detail is to show that we need a less demanding view of reasoning to intention (mine, of course) that covers the relevant ground more smoothly, and does not announce that what seem to be perfectly good examples of such reasoning are in fact not reasoning at all.

It is only in the final two sections that I bring out my defence against Broome's attack on my neo-Aristotelian view of reasoning to an intention.

Broome says that he thinks practical reasoning is much more like theoretical reasoning than I do (2013a: 286). But in my view all that this amounts to is that, like so many others, he understands the practical on a model derived from thinking about the theoretical, whereas I work the other way around. I think that theoretical reasoning is much more like practical reasoning than he does. I start with what he says about the former.

9.1 Broome's Account of Theoretical Reasoning

Broome says that theoretical reasoning is a causal mental process. You start with certain beliefs, and having those beliefs causes you to form a new belief. Such a causal process from beliefs to belief need not be reasoning. For the process to be reasoning, it must satisfy two further conditions. First, you must be conscious of the contents of the beliefs involved; this is not the same as being conscious of your attitude to those contents (in this case, the attitude is belief; in others it will be intention). Second, you must *operate* on those contents in a particular way. In addition to the causal connection between the relevant beliefs, already mentioned, there is also a semantic connection. If the causal process is a process of reasoning, the proposition that is the content of the conclusion-belief must be derived in some way from the propositions that are the contents of the premise-beliefs, and you reason if you 'make the derivation'. This making of the derivation involves tracking a semantic relation, because in making the derivation you are operating on meanings, on the propositions that are the contents of your beliefs. The whole thing is driven by meaning-relations between the premises and the conclusion. Finally, if your 'operation' is reasoning it applies some rule, expressed in a schema or form that links the relevant meanings. Broome thinks of your operation as 'computational or algorithmic' (2013b: 232). But since these terms in their ordinary senses hardly fit some of the examples he gives of reasoning (especially practical reasoning), it is probable that he is using them in a weak sense—as we will see.

I will comment in 9.8 below on the way in which Broome runs together the notions of a proposition, of meanings, and of contents, which are at least potentially distinct. At this stage I want only to suggest that not all the relations between the matters of fact that drive practical reasoning can properly be represented as semantic, on pain of depriving the notion of the semantic of all content. Suppose, for instance, that you recognize that you borrowed the money from her, that she needs to have the money back, and that though you can well use the money you can also easily manage to pay it back—so you (form the intention to) pay it back. Should we allow that the relations between these matters of fact, or between these matters of fact and the intention to repay, are semantic? If they are, are we dealing here with the semantics of English?

Another question is why the whole process is being conceived as causal. No doubt in reasoning one moves (in general but perhaps not exclusively) from things one believes to something else that one believes or hopes or fears or doubts or intends. And one so intends (let's say, picking on that) because of the things from which one reasoned. But is it so obvious that the 'because' here is a causal 'because'? It may be that Broome has simply failed to consider any other possible candidates. But there is one candidate worth considering, that the relevant 'because' is the 'because' of 'for the reason that'. A rational or normative connection of this sort would seem to be perfectly suited to be one that the reasoner is tracking in reasoning, and because of which, or in the light of which, she comes to the conclusion that she does. So, recognizing that reasoning comes in steps, one step to each new consideration adduced and another to the conclusion, we can agree that more is required to link these things together than mere temporal succession. (The various steps must occur in the same person, but this is not enough of a link either.) But that link need be neither semantic nor causal. Similarly, she adduces these considerations rather than those others because these ones are relevant to her purposes, and relevance is a normative relation; so 'because it is relevant' probably does not pick out a standard causal relation either.

Still, with this account of how Broome understands theoretical reasoning, I now turn to consider practical reasoning.

9.2 Broome's Account of Practical Reasoning

So Broome sees theoretical reasoning as an algorithmic causal process grounded in a semantic relation between the propositional contents of one's beliefs. The crucial difference between theoretical and practical reasoning, for him, is that in the latter the reasoner is not operating only on the contents of her beliefs. Practical reasoning is reasoning to intention, and, though intentions do have a propositional content which they can share with beliefs, still belief and intention involve different attitudes to the same content. In theoretical reasoning the only attitude involved is belief, but in practical reasoning the attitude of intention plays a crucial role as well, for we are reasoning to an intention—and in instrumental reasoning we are reasoning from an intention as well. Broome represents a combination of attitude and propositional content thus: <content: attitude>. Reasoning (both theoretical and practical) is a *rule-governed* operation on pairs or complexes of this sort. Such pairs are 'marked contents' in which an attitude attaches its mark to a content.

This is the moment to ask why it is so obvious that reasoning is a rule-governed process. One answer to this question, not available to Broome because of his concentration on the causal, is that reasoning is a normative process, and where there is normativity there must be rules. Another answer is that the examples of theoretical reasoning from which Broome starts are indeed ones for which there is a rule; and he unwarily supposes that this must be true of all processes worth calling reasoning. The matter is important because on the account I have been developing in this book there will be many instances of practical reasoning for which it will be quite impossible to formulate anything worth calling a rule. Consider, for instance, the example from Trollope that I quoted at the end of 3.7. If this passage is allowed to be an instance of reasoning, I defy anyone to find a formulation of the or even a rule that the reasoner might sensibly be supposed to be following. And the same point could be made of the reasonings of most fictional detectives, which are presumably theoretical, at least some of the time. There simply is no rule to be found.

Actually this is not quite true. One can always invent a rule just for the case in hand. For each passage of reasoning '*p*, *q*, so *r*' we can just produce a gerrymandered rule for the case, thus: from *p* and *q* infer *r* (here). But these particularized rules are not the sort of rule that Broome seems to be thinking of. He wants rules that have a kind of general validity, and I suspect that there is not an adequate supply of such rules. (What is more, there is no need for rules if one has the notion of favouring to appeal to—but this comment should really be reserved till later.)

However these things may be, consider now Broome's example of reasoning to intending a necessary means:

I shall attend the conference
If I do not register in advance, I shall not attend the conference
So I shall register in advance

Broome says that the first and the third sentence here express intentions, while the second one expresses a belief. To show this explicitly, we need to reveal the relevant 'marked contents'. Here they are:

<I shall attend the conference:intention>
<If I do not register in advance, I shall not attend the conference: belief>
So <I shall register in advance:intention>

The causal process that takes the reasoner from the first two marked contents to the third is governed by a rule, and the rule is grounded in a rational requirement. That requirement can be expressed roughly thus: rationality *requires* of you that if you intend that p and believe that if not q then not p, you intend that q. The rule, by contrast, *permits* the reasoner to form the conclusion-intention *on the basis of* the combination of the intention-premise and the belief-premise. The rule is a 'basing permission'. (Rational requirements are synchronic: they rule out certain combinations of mental states at a time. Basing permissions are diachronic: they govern the legitimacy of processes, and processes take time.)

The notion of 'basing' is interesting because it bids fair to give us a sense of the 'So:' which we find between the 'premises' and the 'conclusion' in Broomean reasoning, but not in the specification of the relevant rational requirement. The 'So:' means 'based on the above, as is permitted . . .'.

Broome seems to think that all his basing rules (permissions and prohibitions) are grounded in rational requirements. (I say 'seems to' because I will shortly raise doubts about whether he really thinks this.) So the rules that govern practical reasoning, that is, reasoning to intention, are going to be grounded in requirements, and those rational requirements are going to be as tight as possible, so that there is no wriggle room. If you are in breach of one of his requirements, you are to that extent irrational. (Whether we can think of someone as reasoning irrationally, or whether, if she is reasoning, she must be operating in obedience to rational requirements, is a matter that I leave aside. But we might think that if there can be correct reasoning, there must also be such a thing as incorrect reasoning.)

So a process only counts as correct reasoning if it is permitted by a rule that is grounded in a rational requirement. And to lay out the relevant requirement as one that it is irrational to breach, we have to make things maximally tight, and this raises considerable difficulties, with consequent opportunities to exercise ingenuity. The requirement that drives instrumental reasoning, that is, reasoning to a necessary means, fully expressed, comes out as follows (Broome 2013b: 159):

Rationality requires of N that, if

1. N intends at *t* that *e*, and if
2. N believes at *t* that, if *m* were not so, because of that *e* would not be so, and if
3. N believes at *t* that, if she herself were not then to intend *m*, because of that *m* would not be so, then
4. N intends at *t* that *m*.

In this formulation, *e* and *m* are propositions. Given this requirement, there will be a rule expressing a basing permission, thus: one is permitted to base an intention at *t* that *m* on (1) intending at *t* that *e*, (2) believing at *t* that, if *m* were not so, because of that *e* would not be so, and (3) believing at *t* that, if one were not oneself then to intend *m*, because of that *m* would not be so.

Now this is all very complicated, and necessarily so: the complications derive from trying to ensure that if, given (1), (2), and (3), N does not intend at *t* that *m*, N fails to be as rationality requires her to be.[1] I don't know how it would be if we allowed that rationality might merely *commend* certain responses; for Broome, rationality seems to be entirely in the requiring business (though it permits what it does not prohibit, that is, require one not to do). I will be making more of this point below. But for the moment we are working with the supposedly algorithmic/computational conception of the requirements that ground the basing permissions, and our model is Broome's characterization of reasoning to a necessary means to an end that one intends.

---

[1] I originally wrote 'if, given (1), (2), and (3), N does not intend at *t* that *m*, N fails to do what rationality requires her to do'; but that was a mistake. Rationality does not require N to intend that *m* (Broome's version of intending to do something) if (1), (2), and (3) are true; it only requires N to satisfy a complex conditional: to be such that where (1), (2), and (3) are all true, (4) is also true.

It is not clear that he really thinks that *all* basing permissions are grounded in rational requirements. Later he writes:

… correctness in reasoning comes from permission, not requirement.

I mean that correctness does not come directly from requirement. Basing permissions themselves may derive ultimately from requirements. Indeed, there is a reason to think they must. Reasoning is a means of coming to satisfy requirements of rationality. The only way you can come to satisfy the Instrumental Requirement through correct reasoning is by reasoning that is validated by the Instrumental Permission.   (2013b: 258)

But this train of thought is a bit odd. To show that permissions need requirements, we would expect to show not that the permission is the only way of satisfying the requirement—this would seem to show that requirements need permissions—but that the only point of the permission is to satisfy or otherwise support the requirement. Still, perhaps the latter thought is defensible, and if it is, permissions do depend on requirements. But later Broome comes to consider choice in reasoning, as where in order to survive one must either go left or right, but not straight on; this is reasoning to a sufficient means, not a necessary one. And there he says:

There could have been no choice if reasoning were validated by requirements, but actually there is room for choice because it is validated by permissions.
(2013b: 264)

As expressed, the point seems to be just that validation is officially done by permissions, not by requirements, rather than that there is no requirement at issue in the case. But that would be irrelevant. The worry is that there is only choice if there is no requirement at all, and that therefore there can be no such thing as reasoning to a sufficient means. For the discovery of a sufficient means generates no rational requirement that one intend that means. We may have several sufficient means available at once, and so no rational requirement to adopt any particular one of them. And there may be no rational requirement to adopt some one or other of them either—unless we must do so in order to achieve our end, in which case we have the disjunctive thought that taking one or other of the currently available sufficient means is itself a necessary means to our end—which will only be true in special cases. In many cases we might perfectly sensibly wait for a more attractive sufficient means to present itself.

9.3 Broome on Reasoning to a Sufficient Means

To show us how reasoning to a sufficient means is still possible, and sometimes correct, Broome offers us first a 'Generalized Instrumental Requirement' (2013b: 170):

Rationality requires of N that, if

(1) N intends at t that e, and if
(2) N believes at t that, if none of m or n or p or . . . were so, because of that e would not be so, and if
(3) N believes at t that, if she herself were not then to intend m, because of that m would not be so, and if she herself were not then to intend n, because of that n would not be so, and if she herself were not then to intend p, because of that p would not be so . . . , then
(4) N intends at t that m, or intends at t that n, or intends at t that p, or . . .

Suppose now that you are Buridan's ass, fainting with hunger and with indistinguishably delicious piles of hay to left and to right, and that you believe that this is the last moment before you become too weak to go either way, so that if you do not now intend to go left or intend to go right, you will fail to achieve your end, namely survival. You could come to satisfy the Generalized Instrumental Requirement by forming the intention to go left. Your reasoning would be:

I shall survive.
Going either left or right is a means implied by my surviving.
Going left is no worse than going right.
Going left is up to me.
So I shall go left.

This is reasoning, he says, and it is 'intuitively correct', being validated by the following basing permission:

Rationality permits N that:

N intends at some time that e, and

N believes at some time that either *m* or *n* or *p* or... is a means implied by *e*, and

N believes at some time that *m* is no worse a means than *n* or *p* or... , and

N believes at some time that *m* is up to her herself, and

N intends at some time that *m*, and

N's intention that *m* is based on *N*'s intention that *e*, and belief that either *m* or *n* or *p* or... is a means implied by *e*, and belief that *m* is no worse a means than *n* or *p* or... , and belief that *m* is up to her herself. (2013b: 264)

And your reasoning is correct if the intention you form is so based.

9.4 Some Comments

Not all of these comments are criticisms; some are intended only to bring out relevant aspects of Broome's picture.

First, one might question the sense in which such reasoning is 'computational or algorithmic'. By now this demand seems to me to have lost any teeth it originally had. All it means is the (I would say false) view that in all reasoning, theoretical or practical, one is operating on propositions. Consider a slightly expanded version of the reasoning above:

I shall survive.
Going either left or right is a means implied by my surviving.
Going left and going right are equally good.
Going left is up to me, as is going right.
So I shall go left or go right.
So I shall go left.

In what sense is the move from the proposition 'I shall go left or go right' to 'I shall go left' algorithmic or computational? None whatever, I would say, except that it is apparently of the form [p or q: so p], or perhaps better [intend:p or intend:q, so intend:p] or even better [intend:(p or q), so intend:p]. Whichever of these moves we focus on, the process is 'algorithmic or computational' only in the sense that there are some propositions or meanings involved; and that is a vanishingly weak sense of 'algorithmic or computational'.

Second comment: one might wonder whether the 'so' in 'So I shall go left' is a bit bogus; the same 'so' could have taken me to going right. It looks more like a decision than a conclusion of reasoning. The reply to this is that Broome's 'So:' expresses a basing relation, and one is permitted to base an intention to go left on the premises already adduced.

Third comment: there is a difference between a requirement to choose and a required choice. On Broome's account of reasoning to a sufficient means, there is a rational requirement that I choose one of the available means, but no requirement to choose this one rather than that. So the rational requirement is satisfied by choosing—it is a requirement that one choose. There is a permission to choose whichever option one likes.

Fourth comment, longer and less friendly: Broome's structure only applies under certain conditions. The specific form of reasoning to a sufficient means that he gives us, where there is room for choice, is one which only applies if the reasoner is starting from a finite list of options, one of which, she believes, must be taken now or at least intended now if the end is to be achieved, and each of which she believes to be no worse than any other. (This is what we get if we start from the plight of Buridan's ass.) But all of these conditions are special in one way or another, and one could perfectly well imagine that practical reasoning is possible in their absence. For instance, I don't need to think that if I don't form an intention now, I will not achieve my end. I might just think that now is a perfectly good time to address the issue. Second, I would have thought that if one has a list of reasonable options, without any suggestion that that list is exhaustive, one can perfectly well reason to one of them. Third, one does not need to believe, of each option, that it is just as good as any other option there might be, but only that it is good enough. Suppose that I am wondering how to get from Oxford to London for a wedding. I consider various options: the bus, the train, driving, hitching a lift, and so on. I don't need to make my list complete, and I don't need to believe, of the option I select, that there is no better option available. All that rationality requires of me (to put it that way) is that I think that the means which I do select is good enough. Even if I have to believe that none of the other options I have considered is better, I don't have to believe that I have considered all possible options, nor that there is in fact no better option—only (at most) that none such has occurred to me.

In all these ways, Broome seems to me to be forced, by the exigencies of his approach to reasoning in general, to be too restrictive in what he is able to count as practical reasoning.

Fifth comment: One would have naturally thought that the discovery that a projected means is not only necessary but also sufficient for the realization of one's end would strengthen the case for taking that means—as would the discovery, of a sufficient means, that it is also necessary. (I leaned heavily on this point in Chapter 7.) After all, if we think that we won't achieve our end if we don't take this means, and then realize that if we do take that means, we will definitely achieve that end, it seems that we should be even keener to take the means than we were before. (The phrase 'necessary means' is actually a bit misleading in this connection, because it applies to any condition such that, if it fails, we will not achieve our end. So staying alive is a 'necessary means' to almost any end, though it would not normally be thought of as a means at all.)

But Broome is in no position to say anything of this sort. It is impossible to improve on his rational requirement to take a necessary means to one's end. And the permission to select one of the equally good means is actually cancelled, rendered null and void, by the realization that that means is necessary, not merely sufficient. This means that Broome does not escape one of the two criticisms I made in Chapter 7 of any attempt to understand reasoning to a necessary means on the model of *modus tollens*, even though that is not officially what he is doing. He is vulnerable to a complaint analogous to the complaint that it is impossible to improve on *modus tollens*. A case for adopting a means that is based on the fact that the means is necessary, that is, that without it one will fail to achieve one's end, is not improved by finding a Broomean permission to take that means, grounded in a requirement that one take one of the equally good means now.

Sixth comment: There remains the question whether my selection of that option is itself a passage of reasoning. Can I be said to have reasoned to that option if I merely selected it from one of a list of options none of which seemed to me to be better? Or is it that the reasoning has given out once I have determined the nature of the various options on the list, and all that is left is choice? I raised this issue in 8.5, and gave an answer to it there. Here it reappears. It is as much a question for Broome as for me.

So Broome is in no position to press this worry, because he too thinks that there is a way in which the selection of one option among others equally good can in suitable circumstances be the final stage of a process of reasoning.

9.5 A Different Approach

Contrast Broome's account of instrumental reasoning with the one that I would offer. The practical question that the reasoner is faced with is 'How am I to E?', where E is an action, not a proposition. So her question is 'How am I to attend the conference?' She reasons:

(1) If I am to attend the conference, I need to register in advance.
(2) One can register online or on the phone.
(3) Doing it online is easier.
(4) So I'll do that.

The (4) here is supposed to represent the formation of an intention. The intention formed is the intention most favoured by the favourers among the considerations adduced; those considerations favour intending to register online. (Otherwise put: that decision is the right one in the circumstances as given.) And on the account I have suggested, they do this because they favour registering online more than they favour doing it on the phone; this is the Primacy of the Practical. And the same reasoning might have ended in action, if the time had been right. The 'So I'll do that' might have represented a sort of 'So here goes' as she logs on. The reasoning would have been the same either way.

There is one complication that needs to be mentioned at this point, which appeals to the Primacy of the Practical. Normally, the reasons to intend to V are ordinary reasons to V, when the time for V-ing is not yet come. I have my reasons to V, I cannot V yet, and so I form the intention, or decide, to V later, when the opportunity arises. Sometimes, however, there are reasons to make a plan, that is, one needs some plan or other, so one makes a plan. Here part of the reasons for making the plan will be the ordinary reasons for doing the action planned, but others will be reasons for having a plan already made when the time comes.

But this complication makes no real difference. Either way, the intention formed is not, and does not need to be, one whose 'content' stands in some algorithmic relation to the contents of the attitudes expressed by the preceding 'premises', unless the notion of an algorithm is deprived of almost all content—as I have argued above that it already needs to be. The matter is driven entirely by the favouring relation. This distinguishes my account from any account such as Broome's.

This point is independent of the fact that the reasoning in my example is reasoning to a sufficient but not necessary means. Broome's example was of reasoning to a necessary means, though he does not use that term. Instead, he talks more generally of what he calls 'means implied'. A means implied is a consideration such that, if it is not so, because of that one will not achieve one's end. This is a broader notion than that of a necessary means. A means may not be necessary but still be such that if one does not take it, one will not achieve one's end. The example he gives of this is a case where you have the end of getting some milk. You *could* get milk by finding a cow in a field and milking it, but you are not going to do that. The only way you are going to get milk is by buying it in a shop. Buying the milk in a shop is not really a necessary means, but it is, in the circumstances, a means implied by your end.

Broome is surely right about this generalization of the notion of a necessary means, but I will continue to use the terminology of necessary means because of its familiarity. My point here is that it was his concentration on the notion of a necessary means that drove the complexities of his premises (2) and (3)—especially (3). He says that he does not know how to formulate reasoning to the best means to an end that one intends (2013a: 294; 2013b: 170). But a sufficient means need not be thought of as the best; it might just be thought of as good enough. (I am sure that Broome would say that he does not know how to formulate the notion of 'good enough' either.) This should lead one to suspect that his approach generates too stark a difference between reasoning to a sufficient and reasoning to a necessary means. Here I return to the fifth comment in the previous section. How, for instance, could he hope to capture the fact that reasoning to a means that is both necessary and sufficient builds a stronger case for the relevant action than does reasoning to a means that is merely necessary? How could one improve on a valid (or correct) computational derivation?

There are in fact two distinct complaints here. The first is that on his own grounds, Broome ought to maintain that reasoning to a sufficient means is incorrect. For him, the fact that a means is sufficient to achieve one's end makes no case for taking that means at all. This is because it makes no case of the sort that is made by reasoning to a necessary means (on his account of that process). Now in a way he is right about this. If we convert his picture of reasoning to a necessary means appropriately, the rational requirement for reasoning to a sufficient means would be this:

Rationality requires of N that, *if*

(1) N intends at *t* that *e*, and *if*
(2) N believes at *t* that, if *m* were so, because of that *e* would be so, and *if*
(3) N believes at *t* that, if she herself were not then to intend *m*, because of that *m* would not be so, *then*
(4) N intends at *t* that *m*.

And there is obviously no such rational requirement. So, as I say, in a way Broome is right about this. There is never a rational requirement to take a means *merely* because it is sufficient. For we may have a choice of sufficient means, and one is certainly not rationally required to take all of them, or even each of them. And a means may be sufficient but still unattractive in various ways, so that we reasonably decide to hold off until a better one appears. But what this tells us is that making a case for taking a certain means is not properly to be understood in terms of a rational requirement that one breaches if one fails to take that means.

The second complaint, now familiar, is that one would have thought that a case for taking a certain necessary means is made only the stronger if it turns out that that means is also sufficient. But Broome is in no position to show how this is even possible, since one cannot improve on an algorithmically correct process.

A third complaint is that the only forms of reasoning to intention that Broome allows are reasoning from an intended end to intending a (necessary) means to that end, and reasoning from the belief that one ought to V to intending to V. I would want to say that much reasoning to an intention does not start either from an existing intention or from a belief that one ought to do the relevant action. But all such reasonings would be condemned by Broome as incorrect.

9.6 Correct, Sound, and Strong

On my account of reasoning to an intention, it is easy to show how such reasonings might work. They work by adducing considerations that favour acting in the relevant way, and thereby favour intending so to act, if the time for action is not yet come.

Broome is interested in the distinction between correct and incorrect reasoning. All reasoning that is not correct is incorrect, and being correct is not a matter of degree. The distinction between sound reasoning and unsound reasoning is similar in structure, unless soundness is a matter of degree. But there are other terms of appraisal, other contrasts, that I would say are perfectly applicable to reasoning, such as strong vs weak, or more simply better and worse. If we think in the latter terms, we may deny both the existence of and the need for perfect correctness and unimprovable soundness. According to me, reasoning to a sufficient means is often perfectly good reasoning. The fact that this means is sufficient to achieve our end makes something of a case for doing it, and if that means turns out also to be necessary, the case for doing it seems only to get stronger (see 7.4). But the reasoning does not become more correct/sound. Nor does it become closer to a mythical conception of perfect correctness/soundness, any more than an invalid argument that would be valid with two additional premises becomes somehow more nearly valid with the addition of just one of them. There are no such things as degrees of invalidity.

Consider again the example of my trying to work out how to travel to London for the wedding I am attending this weekend. There are various ways in which I can do it. I can go by car, by bus, or by train. Each has its own advantages and disadvantages. Going by car is convenient and fast, but it is expensive and raises parking issues at the other end. Going by bus is cheap and convenient in some ways, but not very flexible, is vulnerable to traffic difficulties, and doesn't take me very near the venue I am trying to reach. The train is more expensive than the bus and is not vulnerable to traffic problems but leaves me even further away from the wedding venue. And so on. Each potential means is sufficient, and none is necessary. And I would think of my attempt to work out which way to get to the wedding as a standard example of (good, sensible) practical reasoning. Admittedly, none of it is 'correct' in Broome's sense. But it is not therefore incorrect. There is nothing wrong with it at all.

9.7 How a Weaker View Can Be Stronger

I have argued that Broome's understanding of practical reasoning led him to be unable to make sense of much of our reasoning to a sufficient means, and also unable to make sense of the way in which the case for taking the necessary means is strengthened if that means turns out also to be sufficient. But there is a way of watering down Broome's emphasis on the algorithmic or computational nature of practical reasoning so as to give him a bit more room for manoeuvre. Whether this would be acceptable to Broome himself is not clear to me; perhaps I should admit that I rather doubt it. But there might be Broomeans out there who are more flexible, to their own advantage. Broome wrote to me (in a private communication), 'I suppose a non-algorithmic operation might involve judgement, say. For instance it might involve the balancing of considerations. Perhaps that's the sort of thing you have in mind for selecting sufficient means. I don't count that as reasoning. I dare say I am using the term more narrowly than many people do.'

Suppose then that we abandon the unnecessarily restrictive idea that all cases of correct reasoning are cases in which the reasoner has a basing permission to operate in a certain way, one that is grounded in a rational requirement. Instead, what we say is that the following is an example of obviously good reasoning (expressed in a way that is amenable to Broome's general approach):

> I shall attend the conference
> If I do not register in advance, I shall not attend the conference
> So I shall register in advance.

And so is this:

> I shall see the latest Bond movie
> If I take Mary to the cinema this evening, I will see the latest Bond movie
> So I will take Mary to the cinema this evening.

In saying that both of these reasonings are good reasonings, we do not try to explain the goodness of the reasonings by appeal to logical structures, or to suitable algorithms. We simply ask you to look at them and to agree that these are sensible ways of going about making a decision, or at least can be in an appropriate context. In this way we avoid the trap that Broome seemed to set for himself, of giving an account of the goodness, or soundness, of reasoning to a necessary means which rendered unsound or incorrect any instance of reasoning to a sufficient means. And we should be encouraged in this policy by noticing that there are plenty of instances of good, sound theoretical reasoning that show no signs of being governed by rational requirements. Rational requirements may then be the core of the explanation of the goodness (or correctness) of some reasoning, but we should not allow this to blind us to the soundness of many other sorts of reasonings which, if forced into a sort of logical shape, would simply look invalid.

This post-Broomean picture has its attractions, mainly a considerable increase in flexibility. It is not really compatible with Broome's talk of the computational and the algorithmic, but perhaps that will just have to be abandoned.

One might still ask how it is that reasoning to a means that is both necessary and sufficient makes a stronger case for taking that means than would either the necessity or the sufficiency, taken alone. Indeed, it is worth pausing to consider whether that is even true. Is the sufficiency of the means an additional reason to take that means, that is, a reason additional to that given us by the necessity of the means? Various answers to this question are possible. One is that it is sometimes so, but not always. Another is that the sufficiency of the means plays a rather different role from that played by its necessity. We might allow that the necessity of the means to an end that one is unwilling to abandon always gives one some reason to take the means. But what if one begins to wonder whether one will ever eventually manage to achieve the end? Any worry of that sort would be silenced by the realization that the means is also sufficient—or that some other means is sufficient. So thoughts about the sufficiency of this, or of some other means are like a barricade, ensuring that our pursuit of the end is not doomed to failure. It is, as Sinan Dogramaci suggested to me, a defeater-defeater. It defeats the possibility of a consideration that prevents us from eventually achieving our end.

This is an interesting suggestion, but perhaps the main point here is that we don't need to say that the fact that the means is sufficient always produces another reason, to add to the one given us by the necessity of the means. All that we really need to say is that we have *more reason* to take the means now that we know it to be both sufficient and necessary, and we don't *have* to explain that claim by supposing that we are dealing with a combination of two independent *reasons*.

9.8 The Content of an Intention

So far I have commented on the complexity and rigidity of Broome's representation of reasoning to an intention to take a necessary means, and also on the difference he must see between reasoning to a necessary and to a sufficient means. I have raised no questions about the way in which he has to understand intention in order to get the whole thing to work. It is one thing to say that he offers an alternative picture of (certain forms of) practical reasoning, one that is inferior to mine if only because it is far less flexible. It is another to say that his account cannot be got to work in its own terms, even in the cases to which his approach might seem best suited. In this section and the next my concern is to decide whether this more direct charge can be brought home.

The main worry in this connection is the way in which Broome thinks of intention as having a proposition as content. He writes:

> The attitudes you reason with—beliefs and intentions for instance—are relations between a person (you) and a proposition. I shall call the proposition the propositional content of the attitude. Attitudes of different types may have the same propositional content.   (2013a: 289)

And he goes on to suggest that the proposition that serves as content for a belief can also serve as content for an intention. It is worth devoting a little attention to this talk of the content of an intention, which I think needs some control. When I say that your belief and my intention have the same content, this might be taken to mean that what you believe is what I intend. But it had better not mean that.

Here we need to be careful. One might say: what I intend is an action, and no action can be what you believe. But what I intend cannot be an action. Admittedly, I have spoken above (on occasions, at least) in terms of intending an action, but that was unwise. In intending now to act later, there is no sense in which the action I go on to perform is *the* action intended. Here we hit the Prichard point again. I cannot intend a particular action; I can only intend to act in a certain way. To put the point somewhat misleadingly: intending can only serve up an action-description to be satisfied by whatever action is done in the service of that intention. Just as a reason to V is not a reason to do some particular action, but only to act in a certain way, or to adopt a certain course of action, so a reason to intend to V (better: a reason to decide to V) is only a reason to form an intention of a certain sort; it does not favour any particular forming of that intention, either. It is a reason to do an intention-forming of a certain sort, namely one with the content 'I will do an action of a certain sort.' The process is doubly indeterminate.

So what we need to say is that what you believe cannot be what I intend, because what I intend is acting in a certain way (and this is not a proposition), and what you believe, whatever such a thing is, does not look capable of being acting in a certain way. So we should not understand Broome's talk of the contents of your beliefs and intentions as talk of *what you believe* and *what you intend*. What then does it mean to say that the proposition is the content of your belief? At one point Broome says that, in reasoning:

> Your operation is computational or algorithmic... You operate on meanings, not on representations. In the example, you operate on the propositions that are the contents of your beliefs. (2013a: 288)

This makes it appear that propositions (or propositional contents) are meanings (without being representations). But if they were meanings, it would be hard for them to be true, since meanings are not among the things capable of truth or falsehood (though *what is meant* is capable of these things). And surely we want the contents of our beliefs to be capable of truth and falsehood, if we are to reason from them or to them. So I think that this suggestion too should be abandoned.

But if so, what are we left with? If propositions are neither meanings nor the things believed, is there some third role for them to play, that of being the 'content' of a belief or an intention? The first sentence in the first of the two passages quoted in this section offers a clue: the attitudes that are so often called propositional attitudes are rightly so called, we might say, because they just are attitudes to propositions. Belief is an attitude that one can take to a proposition: it is the holding-true attitude. Intending is an attitude one can take to a proposition: it is the intending-true attitude. Similarly for other attitudes. The content of fear is a proposition, since fearing is a fearing-true attitude. It does not matter that one cannot fear or hope a proposition, since propositions are not being taken to play the role of what is believed, intended, hoped, or feared. Hoping is a hoping-true attitude.

9.9 Intending and Intending-True

Let us restrict ourselves to intention, which is after all our subject in this chapter. The idea is that when I intend to act in a certain way, what I intend is to act in that way, but intention is itself an attitude of intending-true, an attitude in which I can only stand to a proposition. Does this combination of claims make sense? I doubt it.

There is a different arrangement that I think does make sense, which has it that when I intend to act in a certain way I stand in the intending relation to that (course of) action, or to acting in that way, and I thereby stand in some *other* relation to a proposition; but I do not intend that proposition, I only intend acting in that way. So the intending relation is not itself an intending-true relation, but is always shadowed by such a relation. Similarly for wanting: when I want her to call, what I want is not a proposition (most propositions are not very desirable), but in virtue of wanting her to call I do stand in a relation to a proposition, which we could call the wanting-true relation. In wanting her to call today, I want it to be true that she calls today. So what is involved in wanting it true that she calls today? Well, some people understand this in terms of possible worlds. Just as a proposition can be understood as the class of worlds in which that proposition is true, so wanting it to be true that she calls today can be understood as standing in a certain relation to a class of worlds, namely the class of all worlds in which she calls today. I want the actual world to be one of those worlds. But this is the same class of worlds as the class which is at issue when I intend her to call today. So on this approach in terms of possible worlds, the intending-true relation is not really distinct from the intending-to relation. There is a certain class of worlds, the worlds in which she calls today. Intending her to call, wanting her to call, and believing that she will call are all relations to that class of worlds, but they are three different relations: intending her to call is standing in one relation to that class of worlds, wanting her to call is standing in another relation to that class of worlds, and believing that she will call is standing in a different relation again to that same class of worlds. We are not trying to reduce any of these relations to one of the other two. And there need be no suggestion that that class of worlds is what is wanted, believed, or intended. So with this possible-world understanding of the relevant attitudes, we recover the possibility of revealing the sort of structure that can make a combination of attitudes consistent, in the sort of way that will explain the force of an inference from, say, intention and belief to a new intention.

So far, then, my conclusion is that though Broome is wrong to think of propositions as meanings, and hence wrong to think that the force of reasoning to intention is grounded in semantic relations, there is an understanding of what propositions are and of their role in the account we give of intending, wanting, and believing that will enable him to understand reasoning to an intention in terms of relations between propositions, because it can all be run in terms of relations to worlds in which those propositions are true. But this will be run alongside the admission that intending itself is not a relation to a proposition, or to a class of worlds, but to a way of acting. When I have an intention, what I intend is to act in the relevant way, and in so intending I stand in a certain relation to the class of worlds in which I so act.

Ordinarily, when I intend to V, what I intend is to act in a certain way, and this is the same as to intend acting in that way. I can perhaps also intend that I act in that way. Wanting is a bit different: I can want to V, but I cannot want V-ing, nor want my V-ing, and I cannot want that I V either (or at least any sense given to that phrase would be an arbitrary imposition). What about the actions of others? I can want and intend you to V, and (as I have allowed, with some misgivings) I can intend that you V, but I am not sure that I can intend or want your V-ing. What is the relation between intending to V and intending you to V? One plausible answer is that there is a hidden reflexive place in intending to V, so that in full dress it comes out as intending myself to V. If so, I can intend myself to call just as well as I can intend her to call. But this does not seem right. I can intend to call, and I can intend myself to call, but the attitudes involved are not the same. Intending to call myself is perhaps the same sort of thing as intending to call, since it is like intending to be the one who calls rather than to let others do it, but it is not to be identified with intending myself to call. Why not? In the latter case, intending myself to call, I might try to make sure that I call by making it difficult for myself to avoid doing it—by trying to box myself into a corner, as it were. This is what I might do if I intend her to call (when she doesn't really want to, perhaps); I might try so to arrange things that it would be awkward for her not to call. But I am not standing in that sort of relation to myself when I simply intend to call. If I really intend to do that, I don't need to arrange things so that I don't backslide. So the attitude of intending to V is not the same sort of attitude as that of intending myself to V.

Is the attitude of intending to V the same attitude as that of intending that I V? Again, I would say not, for the same reasons. Intending to V is not really an attitude that sits easily with attempts to make sure that I do in fact V; intending that I V, by contrast, is compatible with boxing myself into a corner to make sure that I do in fact V, since this is just how I would act towards you if I intend that you V.

If this is right, then we should avoid giving exactly the same account of my intending to V and either my intending myself to V, or my intending that I V. Can the possible-world account make room for these differences? Not if it wants to sink all the differences into differences between worlds, since the differences seem to lie more in the relevant attitudes than in the 'content' of those attitudes. But one might think that this need not disconcert Broome. Perhaps all that he needs is to stick to one such attitude, namely that of intending that I V. As long as there is a proposition lurking somewhere within this, (and a possible-world account may provide that) there is going to be some possibility of representing reasoning to intention in terms of marked contents that Broome requires for his system to work.

But the overall result of recognizing the differences between intending to V, intending myself to V, and intending that I V is that there will be large numbers of cases of practical reasoning (reasoning to intention of one form or another) expressed in terms other than intending that I V, and whose soundness Broome will therefore be unable to capture or explain.

Two final points: first, quite a few languages (French and German, for a start) do not even have a way of expressing the idea of intending that p. One wonders how they get on without it, if certain philosophical views are true. By contrast, John Schwenkler reports to me that in Serbian I can only 'intend that I . . .' and cannot 'intend to . . .'. Second, my questions have been questions about the nature of certain attitudes, not about the semantics of certain propositions. And I have not appealed to the point of which Michael Thompson (2008) rightly makes so much, that in English 'I call' (other than in the habitual 'I call my parents every Sunday') does not seem to pick out any proposition at all. There are no truth-conditions for such a thing, as there are for 'I am calling', 'I will call', and so on. And 'I believe that I call her' makes no sense. But I have been allowing that we can discover, or make, a sense for them, by working through the possible-world approach.

9.10 Prior Intention and 'Intention-in-Action'

Theorists of intention have long recognized two distinct contexts in which we speak of intention. We form intentions in advance and wait until the time comes to implement them. But when we act intentionally, we need not have formed a prior intention so to act. We act as we intend, but not necessarily as we intended. The intention which we execute in action need not have been formed in advance.

Recognizing these distinct uses of the notion of intention, a theorist has various options. The first is to suppose that what we have here is really a linguistic accident; the two uses of the notion of intention have little to do with each other. But it seems more attractive to try to relate the two uses to each other somehow. Is it that, when there was a prior intention, and the time for action has now come, the prior intention vanishes, to be replaced with an intention-in-action? Or is it that the prior intention continues throughout the action somehow, ceasing only when the action is done and dusted? And if it does continue, does it somehow get used up as more and more of the course of action intended gets itself done, so that the prior intention fades away to nothing as the action reaches its conclusion? Putting the matter the other way round, is there anything like an intention-in-action to be found before the action starts? The sort of watchful purposiveness and self-guiding that seems to be involved in intentional action doesn't seem to be capable of existence outside of, prior to, the context of action.

Luckily this book is not an attempt to resolve these thorny issues, but that does not mean that we can simply ignore them. When I reason to action, my reasoning serves up an action-description, and I act accordingly. When I do so, I do so intentionally, acting as I intend. I don't need to form a prior intention; I might just act. But Broome's account is primarily aimed at the formation of prior intentions, leaving aside the question whether the action is actually going to get done. How are we to apply Broome's picture to the case where, though the action is intentional, there was no prior intention so to act?

The agent who acts intentionally, but without a prior intention, intends to act and does act; she is acting as she intends, since everything is going successfully. There is a match between how she intends to act and how she is in fact acting.

The problem is that Broome denies, or at least is very close to denying, the possibility of reasoning to an intention-in-action. He thinks we can reason to an intention but not to an action. But this requires a significant distinction between the action and the relevant intention-in-action, so that one can reason to the latter but never to the former. And I would say that no such distinction is available.

9.11 Broome's Argument against an Aristotelian Account

Broome argues that reasoning can take us to the formation of intention, but not all the way to action. It cannot take us all the way to action, because, if it did, any failure to act would be a sort of rational failure. The reasoning would not have been completed properly, since the required conclusion would not have been drawn though the necessary 'premises' are all in place. But rational failures involve breaches of requirements of rationality. And you might well fail to act as you (previously) intended through no rational fault of your own. (They tied you down.) But the failure to intend to act *can* be a rational failure, and would be such a failure when the relevant intention is rationally required of you by the presence and operation of certain marked contents in you, but those marked contents fail to cause the intention. Note the role of the idea of a rational requirement in all this.

Arguing in this way, what is Broome to say about reasoning to an intention-in-action? Is it that the formation of an intention-in-action can be rationally required but the action itself cannot? This seems to impose a distinction between the action meant and the meaning of it. But meaning to act and acting as one means to act are not two distinguishable elements of the intentional action. It is not that an action that one means to do is an act that is accompanied by a sort of meaning—a meaning-to-do, as one might say. We might allow that an intentional action has two aspects: there is the merely physical aspect, and a non-physical aspect. (This would generate a double-aspect account of intention-in-action, a possibility that John McDowell (2015) has brought to our attention recently, building on work by O'Shaughnessy.) But one can only separate the action from the intending, or from the meaning, by thinking of the action as mere bodily motion—as something merely physical. (Moving one's body cannot be thought of as merely physical in this way.) On such a picture, of course one is going to admit that no merely physical change can be the conclusion of reasoning. (Though physical changes can easily end reasoning—death and exhaustion will do this, for a start.) But the act intended is not a mere bodily motion.

This is not all that needs to be said about Broome's argument against my Aristotelian picture. The question is whether one can be rationally required to do something that one is not rationally at fault for not doing. Let us put aside worries about whether rationality issues requirements of this sort and nothing else. Consider moral requirements. Suppose I am morally required to act in a certain way, but they tie me down so that I cannot fulfil those requirements. Have I acted in breach of moral requirements or not? One line is that once they have tied me down, I no longer have those requirements, because ought implies can. But there is another way of thinking of these matters that I find plausible, which is to conceive of a moral requirement to V, fully stated, as the requirement that one V's if one can. The fact that I cannot V does not, on this picture, mean that I am not required to V (if I can). Instead I am prevented from meeting my moral commitments. And we might say the same about rational requirements. I am rationally required to do what I intend to do, if I can.

I have two final points. First, Broome's denial of the possibility of reasoning to an action distorts the focus of our reasons, which is not on intention-forming but on acting. This is the Primacy of the Practical again. Second, if the formation of an intention is the only possible 'conclusion' of deliberation, and we are conceiving this sort of intention as prior intention, rather than as intention-in-action, what happens if the time for action is upon us just as we 'conclude' our deliberation? Is it that, since no prior intention will have been formed, deliberation is subverted, and we must have been engaged in some other procedure? This seems hardly likely.

10

Loose Ends

This short final chapter is an attempt to address a few loose ends and second-order issues.

10.1 Humeanism

I start with a brief attempt to consider to what extent the general approach to reasoning that I offer here is available to those who do not accept the basically realist picture within which it is cast. The question I have in mind here is whether those committed to generally Humean approaches to the philosophy of action are thereby prevented from enjoying the advantages of my post-Aristotelian conception of practical—and thereby of theoretical—reasoning. It might seem that way, because the crux of my story is the favouring relation, and that does not concern itself directly with mental states in the sort of way that a commitment to Humeanism tends to demand. The driving relation for me is one between states of affairs and responses, not between mental states and responses. Worse: I have introduced what is effectively a ban on autobiographical premises: not on all of them, of course, since premises such as 'I am bald' are certainly permitted, indeed encouraged. The ones that are banned are such psychological premises as 'I want a beer', 'my aim is to be top', and 'I believe this is the right way.' And these are the very ones that are dearest to Humeans.

My own view about this latter issue is that the difficulties with those autobiographical premises which I addressed in Chapter 7 were not ones that stemmed from any special approach to the study of human nature, or anything as grand as that. They presented themselves as difficulties for any approach whatever. So there is a shared challenge here. Humeans simply need to say how they propose to deal with it.

The more general issue of the absence of much talk about psychological states cannot be ducked in this way. But Humeans are themselves
well aware that it is not as if our general understanding of human
challenges and achievements in general, or about our rational practice
and response to reasons, is explicitly Humean at the outset. It needs to be
reconfigured in order to be presented in those terms. One way of doing
this would be to distinguish between foreground and background,
in some way such as that offered by Pettit and Smith (1990). In the
foreground are the considerations adduced (such as 'he needs my help');
it is those that we focus on in handling and responding to reasons. But
for each such consideration, there is a psychological state (perhaps one of
recognition of the need for help) operating in the background, understood as an element of the machine that drives the causal process that
is a human being. If any such picture is possible, I see no reason why it
should not be applied to the characterization of human reasoning as I have
given it. Though in reasoning we take ourselves to be—indeed are—moving
from considerations adduced to appropriate responses, this whole story
would then have a Humean background of a now familiar type.

10.2 My Position vis-à-vis the Pragmatist Tradition

The picture I have been trying to promote may remind readers of various
aspects of the pragmatist tradition, and I do not entirely repudiate such
suggestions. Nonetheless I am not convinced that my views fit squarely
into the relevant boxes. Peirce tends to think of reasoning as the attempt
to improve the question with which one started; but, though I am all in
favour of improving questions, I also think of the deliberator as seeking
answers and a new question is not the same as the answer to an old one.
When it comes to action, one has not the luxury of the perpetual
improvement of questions.

Dewey's view that there are no fixed points, and probably no principles either, is one that I am only too happy to echo. It is not, of course,
that there is nothing fixed to adduce, but that the relevance of a consideration adduced is not determinable once and for all in any way that is
immune to shifts in the context. But, like Peirce, Dewey tended to think
that any conclusion we reach is only tenable pro tem—for the while; and

though I can agree that the answer we give to a practical question may be one that we will later regret, and wish to reverse, the fact remains that when it comes to action (rather than to the development of theory) we do need an answer. Any sense of thin ice (and such a sense, we might say, is always more or less appropriate) must be somehow consistent with our ability to choose in the light of reasoning and to act firmly and decisively in accordance with our choice.

10.3 My Relation to Anscombe

Anscombe writes (in *Intention*) that the interest of Aristotle's account of the practical syllogism is that it 'describes an order that is there whenever actions are done with intentions, the same order as I arrived at in discussing what the "intentional action" was, when the man was pumping water. I did not realize the identity until I had reached my results, . . .' (1957: §42). My own view is that her series of 'Why?'-questions, and the A–D structure that emerges in her account of the man pumping water, though entirely characteristic of many intentional actions (more specifically, many of those done neither for their own sakes nor just for a simple reason), is not sufficiently flexible to capture the structure of intentional action as such. So I want to allow that we can represent the reasoning of a detective by means of an Anscombian A–D structure or order of this sort:

(A) if I say to him 'I arrest you', I'll be arresting him; (B) if I arrest him, I'll be arresting the guilty person; (C) if I arrest the guilty person, I'll be solving the crime; (D) if I solve the crime, I'll be promoting the cause of justice, doing my job etc. So I'll say to him 'I arrest you.'

After all, Anscombe does not say that the order is one that is explicitly laid out in any way by the agent. She says only that it 'is there'. I think that this means more than that we can impose it; the discovery of the order is intended to be explanatory, to reveal the intentional nature of the action by unfolding a series of nested answers to 'Why?'-questions.

The question then is whether this order is flexible enough to cover all the cases it needs to cover. More pointedly, one might ask whether an if-then order expressed in Anscombe's way is the only one that will express the way in which an action can be done in the light of reasoning—or if not the only one then still the best. Consider this one:

He had a motive and an opportunity, and there is nobody else of whom the same can be said; further, he gave a false alibi and was identified by the chemist as having asked for rat-poison. So I'll arrest him.

Anscombe should have nothing to say against this structure, though it does not exactly have what she has in mind in speaking of an 'order'. It grows, but it does not grow in the way that her A–D series do. After all, her account of intentional actions as those to which a certain sense of the question 'Why?' is appropriate is perfectly satisfied by these consider-ations, taken severally and together. The only thing she might say beyond this, if she were tempted to say that her own account is uniquely correct as a way of laying out the nature of practical reasoning to action, is that her A–D structure reveals something that my account fails to capture, which she calls 'calculation'. She claims that wherever there is what she was then calling 'practical inference', there is calculation, and by calcu-lation she meant structures built around 'if–then' relations. (One of her examples: if I arrest him, then with the people I have already arrested I will have a whole committee.) My view is more flexible than this. I don't think that practical reasoning *requires* the operation of if–then structures and the sort of calculation that they make possible; I think that such things can happen, but they are only one instance of a more general phenomenon. I would also say that Anscombe's conception of practical inference does not have the flexibility required to make sense of my distinctions between various forms of practical relevance. How, for instance, would she capture the relevance of a 'despite'-clause? How would she capture the relevance of intensifiers and attenuators, of enablers and disablers?

Anscombe's examples are ones in which the agent already has a goal, and is now seeking ways of implementing that plan, working back from it, as it were, to something that is within the agent's capacity *now*. But we also want an account of how we come to form the original plan, such as the plan to get rid of that lot in the house. Practical reasoning is not restricted to the former enterprise. And it is not obvious that an A–D structure is likely to be involved in the decision to find a way of getting rid of that lot, though it might be involved in the choice of a method, once that decision has been made.

A conciliatory position would be to allow that Anscombe has the right account of the cases that interest her, and that are of importance to her in her action of an 'intention with which' one acted, but to insist that there are other forms of practical reasoning than these. The weakness of this position is that it leaves us with a bifurcated account of practical reasoning in general, one semi-inferential in the sense that it reveals a structure that drives the 'inference', the other not really inferential at all since it neither reveals nor depends on any such structure.

Anscombe eventually came to accept that her focus in *Intention* was in danger of being too narrow. She wrote, of her earlier efforts including *Intention*, that they:

represent a struggle to treat all deliberate action as a matter of acting on a calculation how to obtain one's ends. I have now become rather doubtful about this. Of course, it is always possible to force practical reasons into this mould, constructing descriptions of ends like 'not infringing the regulations about traffic lights', 'observing the moral law', 'being polite', 'playing a game according to its rules', and so on. But it now seems to me that there is a contrast between such constructed descriptions of ends, and the means-ends calculations which really do—at least implicitly—take their starting point from some objective which one has. Certain considerations put before me by my friend Georg Henrik von Wright have led me to think this...
(1981: viii)

I think that she means by her phrase 'constructed descriptions' something close to what I was trying to get at with my distinction between substantial and formal ends (7.5). Whether this is so or not, the question for Anscombe is what sort of account she might try to give of those reasonings that are not capable of being 'forced into this mould'. My suggestion is that her account of her favoured cases—the ones she still thinks she was right about—would have to change as well.

10.4 The Primacy of Practical Reason

I have suggested at several places that people have come to distorted views about practical reasoning because they approach it with misconceptions derived from prior study of theoretical reasoning. (Even Aristotle made this mistake, in supposing that all practical reasoning is syllogistic.) By contrast, my picture derives largely from thinking about practical reasoning, and then applying the results to theoretical reasoning, where it turns out that the relations unearthed in our enquiries into practical reasoning are still perfectly appropriate, and retain all their explanatory power.

But does this amount to any position worth calling the Primacy of Practical Reason? Is there anything more here than a deep similarity, with no asymmetries of the sort that would justify talk of Primacy? Even if we added that some things have proved easier to discern in the practical context than in the theoretical, ease of access is one thing and anything worth calling Primacy is another.

So do I want to say, with Kant (in the Preface to the *Groundwork*), that all rationality is in the end practical? I certainly want to agree broadly with Joseph Raz's remark, many years ago, that in believing we are as active as we ever are. I think that there is a perfectly good notion of deciding that things are thus and so, where deciding what is so is the theoretical analogue of deciding what to do. And I would resist post-Humean suggestions that believing is a state that just happens to you, in favour of a notion of judgement in which the judger is manifestly active, an agent rather than a recipient. In taking belief as an active response to considerations adduced, we are allowing that the contemplative conception of the theoretical is a distortion, and that in all thinking we are operating as agents.

Perhaps the bottom line here is a conception of ourselves as normatively sensitive agents, capable of responding to reasons as reasons wherever they are to be found. A reason is a reason for a response, and in responding we are active; we are not pushed about by reasons (as if by our desires, say), but respond to them as calling for this rather than that from us. The connection between reason and response is quite different from the connection between cause and effect. The former is normative.

10.5 Propositions

How would things look if we decided that propositions can in fact favour responses, contrary to what I argued in 2.6? Such a decision would have to be implemented on both sides of the practical/theoretical distinction. Propositions will have to be reasons for action as well as for belief.

I recognize that my view that propositions can favour nothing is not among my most popular suggestions. Nonetheless, one of the main ways in which I came to the views here presented was by rejecting the centrality of the trio inference-premise-conclusion, and the role that propositions play in our conception of that trio. This rejection made room for the idea that that which one can reason to might be a response rather than a proposition, and so an action as easily as it could be a belief. If what one reasons to must be a proposition, the cause of genuinely practical reasoning is in danger of being lost. But there is also the question of what one reasons from. If one reasons from propositions, the things one reasons to must be things that can enter into the sort of relations that propositions can enter into. And it seems that only propositions can enter into those relations—unless one also allows beliefs in there, by courtesy, as it were. Not action, anyway.

My aim in all this was to promote the idea that it is believings and actings that are favoured by what does the favouring. So long as the friend of propositions will allow that among the responses that propositions can favour there will be actions as well as beliefs, nothing is lost.

But there is a dreadful tendency to suppose that once we cast the favourers as propositions, the relations that drive reasoning will be the familiar inferential relations of necessitating and probabilifying, where what is necessitated or probabilified is not a belief but the truth of a proposition. And it was by rejecting the primacy of inference that I had hoped to make progress. I do not infer believing that q from believing that p; but in reasoning I pass from believing that p to believing that q, in a way that can be analogous to passing from believing that p to acting in a certain way.

As long as such errors are avoided, it seems to me that it is just possible for me not to insist on my own views about propositions and their ability to favour responses. But I will also have to take some attitude to the idea that in theoretical reasoning I reason from things believed (understood as propositions) to things to be believed, and so in practical reasoning I reason from things believed to things to be done. And here I become deeply uncomfortable, because an attachment to the nexus of propositions will have us say that, if one can reason to a thing to be done, such a thing must still be a proposition, and this last seems to me very hard to sustain.

10.6 My Full View

This is an overall summary of my position, one of many helpful comments from Kurt Sylvan on an earlier draft:

Your full view is the conjunctive view that (i) we can reason directly to actions and (ii) this is not elliptical reasoning in which prior steps (normative belief, intention) are omitted, but (iii) is in fact reasoning that omits no prior steps precisely because practical reasons are only directly reasons for action, and are indirectly reasons for intentions and normative beliefs. These pieces are all separate. One could also imagine a view, for example, on which (i) and (ii) are held, but we hold that there is nothing enthymematic about any of the direct moves from (a) reason to action, (b) reason to intention, and (c) reason to normative belief.

But in fact my view is that though certain theoretical reasons are reasons for belief because they are reasons for action, and the same applies to certain reasons to intend, this need *not* mean that reasoning to those 'conclusions' is always enthymematic (in the sense of 'leaving something out'). A derivative normative status need not require that all reasoning to those conclusions is similarly derivative in the sense of being enthymematic if the relevant derivation is not explicitly included. The Primacy of the Practical does not commit one to maintaining that all reasoning is primarily to action and only secondarily to belief or to intention. It is a primacy in the order of explanation rather than in the structure of reasoning.

References

Alvarez, M., and Hyman, J. (1998) 'Agents and their Actions', *Philosophy* 73, pp. 219–45.

Anscombe, G. E. M. (1957) *Intention* (Oxford: Basil Blackwell).

Anscombe, G. E. M. (1974) 'Von Wright on Practical Inference', in P. A. Schilpp, ed., *The Philosophy of Georg Henrik von Wright* (La Salle, Ill.: Open Court Publishing); reprinted as 'Practical Inference' in R. Hursthouse et al., eds, *Virtues and Reasons: Philippa Foot and Moral Theory* (Oxford: Clarendon Press, 1995), pp. 1–34.

Anscombe, G. E. M. (1981) *Collected Philosophical Papers*, vol. 3 *Ethics, Religion and Politics* (Minneapolis: University of Minnesota Press).

Audi, R. (2006) *Practical Reasoning and Ethical Decision* (London: Routledge).

Broome, J. (2004) 'Reasons', in R. J. Wallace et al., eds, 2004: 28–55.

Broome, J. (2013a) 'Practical Reasoning and Inference', in B. Hooker et al., eds, *Thinking about Reasons* (Oxford: Oxford University Press), pp. 286–309.

Broome, J. (2013b) *Rationality Through Reasoning* (Oxford: Wiley Blackwell).

Chisholm, R. M. (1963) 'Supererogation and Offence', *Ratio* 5, pp. 1–14; reprinted in his *Brentano and Meinong Studies* (Atlantic Highlands, NJ: Humanities Press, 1980), pp. 98–113.

Coope, U. (2007) 'Aristotle on Action', *Proceedings of the Aristotelian Society* supp. vol. 81, pp. 109–38.

Dancy, J. (1983) 'Ethical Particularism and Morally Relevant Properties', *Mind* 92, pp. 530–47.

Dancy, J. (1993) *Moral Reasons* (Oxford: Basil Blackwell).

Dancy, J. (2000) *Practical Reality* (Oxford: Clarendon Press).

Dancy, J. (2004a) *Ethics Without Principles* (Oxford: Clarendon Press).

Dancy, J. (2004b) 'Enticing Reasons', in R. J. Wallace et al., eds, 2004: 91–118.

Dancy, J. (2015) 'Reasons for Broome', in A. Reisner et al., eds, *Weighing and Reasoning* (Oxford: Oxford University Press), pp. 177–88.

Fernandez, P. A. (2016) 'Practical Reasoning: Where the Action Is', *Ethics* 126, pp. 869–900.

Grice, P. (2001) *Aspects of Reason* (Oxford: Oxford University Press).

Harman, G. (1986) *Change in View* (Cambridge, Mass.: Bradford Books).

Hornsby, J. (2013) 'Basic Activity', *Proceedings of the Aristotelian Society* 87, pp. 1–18.

Hyman, J. (2015) *Action, Knowledge, and Will* (Oxford: Oxford University Press).

Kearns, S., and Star, D. (2009) 'Reasons as Evidence', in R. Shafer-Landau, ed., *Oxford Studies in Metaethics* vol. 4. (Oxford: Oxford University Press), pp. 215–42.

Kenny, A. J. P. (1975) *Will, Freedom and Power* (Oxford: Basil Blackwell).

Lowe, J. (2008) *Personal Agency* (Oxford: Oxford University Press).

McDowell, J. (2015) 'Acting as One Intends', in J. Dancy and C. Sandis, eds, *Philosophy of Action: An Anthology* (Oxford: Wiley Blackwell), ch. 15, pp. 145–57.

Nozick, R. (1968) 'Moral Complications and Moral Structures', reprinted in his *Socratic Puzzles* (Cambridge, Mass.: Harvard University Press, 1997), ch. 10.

Paul, S. (2013) 'The Conclusion of Practical Reasoning: The Shadow Between Idea and Act', *Canadian Journal of Philosophy* 43.3, pp. 287–302.

Pettit, P., and Smith, M. (1990) 'Backgrounding Desire', *Philosophical Review* 99, pp. 564–92.

Pollock, J. (1994) 'Justification and Defeat', *Artificial Intelligence* 67.2, pp. 377–407.

Price, A. W. (2008) *Contextuality in Practical Reason* (Oxford: Clarendon Press).

Price, A. W. (2011) *Virtue and Reason in Plato and Aristotle* (Oxford: Clarendon Press); esp. §X.

Prichard, H. A. (1912) 'Does Moral Philosophy Rest on a Mistake?', *Mind* 21, pp. 21–37; reprinted in Prichard 2002: 7–20.

Prichard, H. A. (1932) 'Duty and Ignorance of Fact', *Proceedings of the British Academy*; reprinted in Prichard 2002: 84–101.

Prichard, H. A. (2002) *Moral Writings*, ed. J. MacAdam (Oxford: Oxford University Press).

Quinn, W. (1993) 'Putting Rationality in its Place', in his *Morality and Action* (Cambridge: Cambridge University Press), pp. 228–55.

Raz, J. (1975a) 'Reasons for Action, Decisions and Norms', *Mind* 84, pp. 481–99.

Raz, J. (1975b) *Practical Reason and Norms* (London: Hutchinson).

Raz, J., ed. (1978) *Practical Reasoning* (Oxford: Oxford University Press).

Raz, J. (2011) *From Normativity to Responsibility* (Oxford: Oxford University Press).

Raz, J. (2015) 'Normativity: The Place of Reasoning', in *Philosophical Issues* 25.1: Normativity, pp. 144–64.

Rödl, S. (2007) *Self-Consciousness* (Cambridge, Mass.: Harvard University Press).

Ross, Sir David (1930) *The Right and The Good* (Oxford: Clarendon Press).

Scanlon, T. M. (2014) *Being Realistic about Reasons* (Oxford: Oxford University Press).

Seidman, J. (2005) 'Two Sides of Silencing', *Mind* 55, pp. 68–77.

Stocker, M. (1968) 'Duty and Supererogation', *American Philosophical Quarterly* Monograph #1, pp. 53–63.

Tenenbaum, S. (2007) *Appearances of the Good* (Cambridge: Cambridge University Press).

Thompson, M. (2008) *Life and Action* (Cambridge, Mass.: Harvard University Press).

Thomson, J. J. (2008) *Normativity* (Chicago and La Salle, Ill.: Open Court), esp. Addendum 4.

Toulmin, S. (1956) *The Uses of Argument* (Cambridge: Cambridge University Press).

Toulmin, S. ed. with A. Janik and R. Rieke (1979) *An Introduction to Reasoning* (New York: Macmillan).

Von Wright, G. H. (1963) 'Practical Inference', *The Philosophical Review* 72, pp. 159–79; reprinted in Von Wright 1983: 1–17.

Von Wright, G. H. (1972) 'On so-called Practical Inference', *Acta Sociologica* 15, pp. 39–53; reprinted in Von Wright 1983: 18–34.

Von Wright, G. H. (1983) *Practical Reason* (New York: Cornell University Press).

Wallace, R. J., Pettit, P., Scheffler, S., and Smith, M., eds (2004) *Reason and Value: Themes from the Moral Philosophy of Joseph Raz* (Oxford: Clarendon Press).

Index

requirements: rational 117, 149–52, 154,
     157–8, 168; moral, 169
Rödl, S. 109, 121
Ross, Sir W. D. 48n, 84

Scanlon, T. 36
Schwenkler, J. 166
Seidman, J. 115
silencing 115
Smith, M. 171
so 15
speculative reasoning *see* reasoning,
     practical vs theoretical
Star, D. 93n
Stocker, M. 31n
Sylvan, K. 102n, 176–7

Tenenbaum, S. 28n
'that's it' clause 140–2

Thompson, M. 166
Thomson, J. Jarvis 90–4
Toulmin, S. 56n, 65; on data, warrant,
     backing, rebuttal, qualifier 46–9
Trollope, A. 57
truth 97–8

unity of practical and theoretical
     reason 1–2

value: as the explanation of practical
     reasons 98–9; truth as a value 97–8;
     probability as a value
     100–1
Von Wright, G. H. 23, 174

weighing 3, 27–8
Wodak, D. 7n, 105
Wollheim, R. 107, 108